The Leaky Bucket

What's Wrong with Your Fundraising and How You Can Fix It

Ellen Bristol
Linda Lysakowski, ACFRE

The Leaky Bucket: What's Wrong with Your Fundraising and How You Can Fix It

One of the **In the Trenches™** series

Published by
CharityChannel Press, an imprint of CharityChannel LLC
30021 Tomas, Suite 300
Rancho Santa Margarita, CA 92688-2128 USA

charitychannel.com

ISBN Print Book: 978-1-938077-13-5 | ISBN eBook: 978-1-938077-33-3

Library of Congress Control Number: 2013939558

13 12 11 10 9 8 7 6 5 4 3 2 1

Printed in the United States of America

What People Are Saying about *The Leaky Bucket* . . .

I'm delighted to see The Leaky Bucket: What's Wrong with Your Fundraising and How You Can Fix It *available to us. It's a much-needed resource and a very welcome one.*
    Andrew Watt
    CEO, AFP International

With a highly practical style and clear tips, this quick read is a helpful guide for both experienced and novice fundraisers. The chapter on fundraising diversification, "Too Many Eggs, Too Few Baskets," is especially useful for reminding nonprofit professionals to think strategically, focus on abundance, and access multiple capacity-building streams from various funders. Making years of wisdom so accessible to fundraisers everywhere makes an important contribution to the capacity of the sector.
    Scott Bechtler-Levin
    CEO, IdeaEncore

The Leaky Bucket: What's Wrong with Your Fundraising and How You Can Fix It *integrates the best of business management tools with the best practices of fundraising to provide a needed, timely, and effective resource. In the changing landscape of funding with myriad challenges,* working smartly to do good well is essential. *The fresh perspective prompted by the questions raised and solutions offered by two skilled professionals can take your organization from treading water or sinking to full steam ahead. It is practical, accessible, and more of an in-depth conversation with you and your organization than one more "how to" book of tactics and strategies.*
    Mary A. Brumbach, PhD, CFRE
    Executive District Director of Strategic Funding
    Dallas County Community College District
    Dallas, Texas

Linda and Ellen are great together. Their knowledge and expertise in the nonprofit sector and their advice and caring words truly inspire many nonprofits worldwide. They have so much to offer, and it's always a pleasure to help them spread the good word. Any nonprofit looking for a shot of "can do" and energy would be wise to read their book!

Declan Murphy
Marketing and Social Media Coordinator
GiftWorks

I wish I'd had The Leaky Bucket: What's Wrong with Your Fundraising and How You Can Fix It *when I first started my development career. Insider tips and techniques combined with common-sense applications add up to a phenomenal blueprint that should be required reading by every fundraising or development professional.*

Lynne Viccaro O'Leary
Vice President—Marketing
Teachers Federal Credit Union (TFCU)

When Ellen asked me to read The Leaky Bucket: What's Wrong with Your Fundraising and How You Can Fix It, *I was already a fan. Now that I've read it, I understand why this book is so valuable. In it, Ellen and Linda explain the critical best practices of fundraising in an artful and accessible way. Their insights have helped our board press the "reset" button and start over the right way. I'm telling all my nonprofit colleagues, "This is the book you have to buy next."*

Elly Du Pre
Executive Director
Lighthouse of Broward
Fort Lauderdale, Florida

Publisher's Acknowledgments

This book was produced by a team dedicated to excellence; please send your feedback to editors@charitychannel.com.

We first wish to acknowledge the tens of thousands of peers who call charitychannel.com their online professional home. Your enthusiastic support for the **In the Trenches**™ series is the wind in our sails.

Members of the team who produced this book include:

Editors

Acquisitions Editor: Stephen Nill

Comprehensive Editor: Stephen Nill

Copy Editor: Jill McLain

Production

In the Trenches Series Design: Deborah Perdue

Layout Editor: Jill McLain

Administrative

CharityChannel LLC: Stephen Nill, CEO

Marketing and Public Relations: John Millen

About the Authors

Ellen Bristol

Ellen Bristol, president of Bristol Strategy Group, works with nonprofit organizations to improve their fundraising effectiveness, raise income, and involve their boards more effectively. She is widely known for her innovative work in developing management controls, processes, benchmarks, and other guidelines, exemplified by her trademarked methodology Fundraising the SMART Way™ and her popular assessment tool The Leaky Bucket Assessment for Effective Fundraising™, which inspired the writing of this book. Ellen likes to say, "We bring you the science that makes the art of fundraising possible."

Ellen has an unusual background for such an influential fundraising expert: she spent nearly twenty years selling mainframe computers before establishing her consulting practice in 1995 and has never worked for a nonprofit organization. She launched Bristol Strategy Group with a mission to adapt the benefits of formal process management to the field of corporate sales but quickly realized that her passion lay in the social sector. Nonprofit executives from all over the United States, Canada, the United Kingdom, China, and even the Galapagos Islands have benefited from completing the Leaky Bucket Assessment.

Ellen, who launched her first business, a day-care program, at age 14, graduated from Columbia University with a degree in English literature. Her first paid job was as an avant-garde modern dancer. She had a short career as a magazine editor before launching her career in information technology.

She currently serves on the board of her local AFP chapter, AFP Broward (Florida), and is a member of the Professional Advancement Division of

AFP International, where she sits on the Research Council. In addition to her work with AFP, Ellen is a member of the Florida Speakers Association, the Association of Psychological Type, and the Broward County Chamber of Nonprofit Organizations. She is a regular volunteer teacher at LEAP for Ladies, a local program providing training in business skills and entrepreneurship to women in prison.

Linda Lysakowski, ACFRE

Linda Lysakowski, ACFRE, is one of approximately one hundred professionals worldwide to hold the Advanced Certified Fund Raising Executive designation. In her twenty years as a philanthropic consultant, Linda has managed capital campaigns ranging from $250,000 to more than $30 million, helped hundreds of nonprofit organizations achieve their development goals, and trained more than 25,000 professionals in Canada, Mexico, Egypt, Bermuda, and most of the fifty United States in all aspects of philanthropic development.

Linda has received the Outstanding Fundraising Executive award from both the Eastern Pennsylvania and the Las Vegas chapters of AFP (Association of Fundraising Professionals). In 2006, Linda was recognized internationally with the Barbara Marion Award for Outstanding Service to AFP.

Linda is a graduate of Alvernia University with degrees in banking and finance and theology/philosophy and a minor in communications. As a graduate of AFP's Faculty Training Academy, she is certified as a Master Teacher. She is a member of the board of directors of the AFP Foundation and past president of the AFP Sierra Chapter in Reno, Nevada. She is a frequent presenter at regional and international conferences and has received two AFP research grants.

Linda is the author of *Recruiting and Training Fundraising Volunteers*; *The Development Plan*; *Fundraising as a Career: What, Are You Crazy?*; *Capital Campaigns: Everything You NEED to Know*; *Raise More Money from Your Business Community*; *Fundraising for the GENIUS*; *Are You Ready for a Capital Campaign?* (workbook); a contributing author to *The Fundraising Feasibility Study—It's Not About the Money*; coeditor of *YOU and Your Nonprofit* and *The Nonprofit Consulting Playbook*; and coauthor of *The Essential Nonprofit Fundraising Handbook*. Contact Linda at www.lindalysakowski.com.

Authors' Acknowledgments

This book is dedicated to the hundreds of nonprofit leaders, founders, executives, and board members who have completed the Leaky Bucket Assessment and bravely shared their results, no matter how gruesome. The work I have been privileged to do with you has taught me so much about the power of nonprofit organizations and the challenges they endure in order to serve the greater good.

I would also like to acknowledge the generosity and encouragement that my coauthor, Linda, and my publisher, Steve Nill, have afforded me. Without you, this book would never have been written.

Ellen Bristol

I would like to thank the many fundraisers and board members who have attended my workshops, conferences, and webinars over the past twenty-five years. There have been more than 25,000 of you! Many of you have shared with me what's been wrong with your fundraising and, together, we've brainstormed on how to fix these wrongs.

Thank you for being brave enough to share your frustrations and questions, and thank you for being willing to take the leap of faith that has helped you grow stronger fundraising programs. I hope this book will help you continue to grow and improve your nonprofits.

Linda Lysakowski

Contents

Foreword

The fundraising environment in which we're operating today is very different from the one that many of us experienced when we came into the profession. The pace of change is exponential. The economic and social environment is experiencing a degree of volatility that few of us have seen in our lifetimes before—and that's unlikely to change. Governments are pulling back from social investment while the demand for the services our organizations offer is great and will only grow greater and greater. Levels of giving have been underwhelming in recent years, and it will be some years before they recover to the levels of 2007 and before—and, at 2 percent of GDP, it could be argued that giving has remained flat over much of the last fifty years. There has never been a time when we have had greater need to achieve impact in our careers and for the causes we support.

So what does happen five years out? What happens as you progress through your career and need to evaluate the impact of what you are doing or assess your plans for future campaigns? How do you evaluate what's appropriate for your organization at its specific stage of maturity? And, if you're not a fundraiser but a member of the board, how do you assess the degree of success that your development office is achieving for you? How do you stay at the top of your game?

Linda Lysakowski and Ellen Bristol have many years of fundraising experience between them. Both have experienced these dilemmas and many more. And both have helped others work through these scenarios as fundraisers, authors, and educators themselves.

This new joint venture, *The Leaky Bucket: What's Wrong With Your Fundraising and How You Can Fix It*, draws on Linda and Ellen's deep understanding of the fundraising environment and uses it to help us address these challenges. It helps shine a spotlight on our own efforts and those of our team and assess the likely level of impact they will have.

Linda and Ellen provide us with the framework we need, first to assess the effectiveness of our fundraising programs and then to determine what's needed to bring them to a successful conclusion. They help us understand the impact of the bond between staff and volunteer and how to ensure the success and achievement of both. And they direct us to the resources that all of us need to do that.

I'm delighted to see *The Leaky Bucket: What's Wrong With Your Fundraising and How You Can Fix It* available to us. It's a much-needed resource and a very welcome one.

Andrew Watt
President and CEO
Association of Fundraising Professionals
Fellow, Institute of Fundraising

Introduction

Why We Wrote This Book

When the two of us met, we recognized instantly that we shared a common bond. Both of us had come from the corporate sector, both of us had a passion for the nonprofit sector, and each of us had been bringing our business skills to the nonprofit world for more than twenty years. And, most importantly, each of us wanted to do even more to help nonprofits learn how to use the assessment tools businesses have been using for years to help them improve results.

In our very first conversation, we talked about various tools we've used to help nonprofits assess their effectiveness. Ellen described her Leaky Bucket Assessment to Linda this way: "It's a great way to find out what's wrong with your fundraising." Linda responded, "Hey, that's a terrific subject for a book! Let's write it together." So we did. We knew that many things can go wrong in fundraising, some of which are not under our control. But we also know that fundraising organizations tend to lack certain basic practices that could improve performance significantly, including the nine areas measured by the Leaky Bucket Assessment as well as other tools each of us has used in our consulting practices. And since we agreed that it's a whole lot easier to fix it before it's broken than it is to clean up the mess afterward, we wrote this book as a labor of love.

The Leaky Bucket: What's Wrong with Your Fundraising and How You Can Fix It is the natural outgrowth of our mutual desire to help nonprofits understand why some of their fundraising efforts fail and to help them make the necessary corrections in what they are doing. We want your nonprofit to have one of the solid, watertight development programs that will enable you to change the world!

As you read this book, we hope you will take an honest, objective look at your development program. And that when you finish this book, you will have a plan for a stronger, more efficient, and more effective development program.

Chapter One

The Leaky Bucket Assessment for Effective Fundraising

IN THIS CHAPTER

···→ Why knowing what's wrong with your fundraising is so important

···→ About the Leaky Bucket Assessment

···→ What we have discovered about fundraising effectiveness, efficiency, and productivity

···→ A summary of best practices to improve your fundraising efforts

Let's start this book with a basic question. How is your fundraising going—really?

Whenever we ask that question, we're likely to get one of two different answers, each of which has innumerable variations.

◆ Answer #1: We're doing *great*!

◆ Answer #2: OMG, we're doing *terrible*!

If you really are doing great in all respects, then you deserve accolade upon accolade. You're doing the right things the right way at the right time, and it's paying off.

Unfortunately, some of those who chose Answer #1 might be disregarding (or denying) some of the not-so-great stuff that's really going on in their fundraising efforts. So they chase prospects that are already dead on arrival, thus reducing the "net profit" (if you'll excuse the term) of the whole initiative. Or they can't resolve the challenges of getting the board involved, have poor metrics for measuring and managing performance of the development staff, or lack reliable insights into the actual returns of various campaigns or initiatives. Or maybe levels of funding diversification are out of balance. Sometimes Answer #1 really means "We're doing great, as long as we don't look at what it's costing us to get our results, and we define 'great' very narrowly."

Answer #2, by contrast, could mean "If we don't get some money *soon*, we'll have to close our doors." Or it might just mean "We haven't figured out the challenges of getting the board involved, we have lousy metrics for measuring and managing performance of the development staff, and we're never really sure if our campaigns and initiatives are paying off. Plus, our levels of funding diversification are out of balance."

Gee. Sounds just like Answer #1.

Let's face it. We don't have many reliable ways to define what we mean by effective or productive fundraising, so we're stuck with anecdotes and war stories. We need a way to figure out what it takes to make the fundraising function workable. This problem has been bugging us for years, so Ellen's company Bristol Strategy Group launched an online assessment in the spring of 2011, for the purpose of bringing some clarity and science to the topic: the Leaky Bucket Assessment for Effective Fundraising. It measures the level of maturity of nine key practices that either contribute to or detract

---

Ellen designed the Leaky Bucket Assessment as a quick, informal way to measure the level of maturity of nine basic business practices that development shops need to have in place. She thought that it would be just for fun and give people something to talk about. At the time of writing, however, about four hundred individuals have participated, and the findings have been surprising. We talk about these findings in the following chapters.

See **Appendix B** for a link to the Leaky Bucket Assessment for Effective Fundraising.

 practical tip

from fundraising effectiveness and productivity. And, so far, the findings are pretty interesting.

Fundraising and Performance Metrics

In fundraising, performance tends to be measured by a single metric—how much money flows in the door, a classic "trailing indicator" if there ever was one. When you measure only trailing indicators, the information comes in too late—after the process is complete—to alert you to a needed change in course. Sometimes development shops also measure activity, like the number of grant applications or major gift proposals produced, number of direct-mail pieces sent, number of RSVPs for the annual gala, and the like. It's better than measuring nothing, but when you measure activity, you find out only how much activity you've produced. The link between activity and results is weak.

Good process management is highly effective at identifying and repairing the cost, waste, and rework that used to plague manufacturing plants. Ever since the 1950s, process management techniques have been widely used in manufacturing and other industries. They cut down waste, rework, and other drains on productivity by scrutinizing all steps and inputs to the process, identifying the root causes of errors and mistakes, and changing things upstream to get better results at lower costs downstream. Continual repetition of these disciplines brings about substantial reductions in cost and time and reveals unexpected opportunities for innovation. In fact, you can observe the benefits of process management disciplines just by walking into any office-supply store.

> A trailing or lagging indicator is an indicator that is observed at the tail end of a process. Since income appears after the cultivation process, it is a trailing indicator.
>
> A leading indicator is an indicator that occurs in the early or middle stage of the same process. A leading indicator in fundraising could be "prospect asks for proposal."

Definition

As recently as the early 1990s, if you needed extra space to store files in your computer, it could cost $50,000 to buy clumsy devices the size of a refrigerator, and you would be able to store only about as many files as you could stash in one drawer of a filing cabinet. Not to mention the computer would fill up a whole room and you'd have to spend years figuring out how to use it, and you'd have to order the storage devices—and the computer—custom-made. These days, you can pick up a four gigabyte thumb drive for about twenty bucks at any office-supply store. That's probably enough room to store an encyclopedia.

In case you haven't checked recently, we haven't really made equivalent advances in the world of fundraising. Waste (chasing unqualified prospects), rework (acquiring unprofitable and high-maintenance grants, major donors, or corporate sponsors), and other unacknowledged drains on productivity tend to persist in many fundraising organizations. When this is the case, the nonprofit may easily fail, or at least fail to thrive, in spite of motivating missions and decent, even marvelous, programs and services. Sure, we have better donor-management software applications, but don't expect your software to fix a process that's broken or poorly defined. It just doesn't work.

The Leaky Bucket Assessment measures these nine business practices:

◆ How you qualify donor/grantor prospects

◆ How you acquire new donors

◆ How you retain donors

◆ How you upgrade donors through "up-selling" and "cross-selling"

◆ How you manage funding diversification

◆ Your staff resources for fundraising

◆ How you measure fundraising performance

◆ What you include in your fundraising tool kit

◆ What techniques you use when fundraising results fall below desired levels

deﬁnition

What's the point of this history lesson? We wanted to give you an approach to managing your fundraising organization and practices that would create more clarity, give you better insights, and improve your ability to hold the development team accountable for results. Let's start with what the Leaky Bucket Assessment measures.

The assessment ranks your fundraising program at one of four levels of maturity. Since productivity tends to leak out of development organizations in ways we don't see until the pipes break, we use these four highly scientific titles:

◆ Leaking Like a Sieve!

◆ Call the Productivity Help Line!

◆ Time for Preventive Productivity Maintenance!

◆ Watertight!

To our dismay, very few nonprofit organizations came in at the Watertight level. The vast majority—about 79 percent overall—came in with scores at the two lowest levels.

Our friend Larry completed the assessment. Larry has decades of success in the for-profit world, so we thought his organization would get pretty good scores. But we were wrong. Larry is the chief operating officer of a local social services agency that runs a $4 million budget every year. Its principal source of income is contracts with federal agencies. Larry and the rest of the management team are really worried about the agency's sustainability, since those federal contracts are going to sunset one day in the foreseeable future, and the fates of hundreds of clients lie in the balance. After completing his assessment, Larry said, "I *know* these are basic best-practices for any business! But we simply don't have any of them in place today!"

Let's take a look at the results we've seen from the Leaky Bucket Assessment to date.

Overall Productivity/Effectiveness Results

How many times have you heard those familiar complaints and war stories? You know the ones:

◆ The board just doesn't get it.

◆ I'm supposed to write grant applications, cultivate major donors, do all the marketing, *and* update the website!

◆ Programs couldn't bring in enough clients, so the grantor's not renewing us at the same level. And now they're saying it's *my* fault!

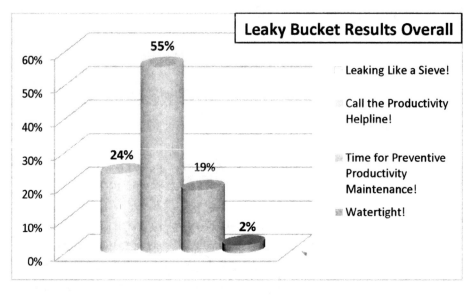

Well, Ellen thought, "We hear this stuff so often, maybe there's something to it." And she was on target. Take a look at the results of the Leaky Bucket study. First, we collated the total scores of all participants to date. This graph shows how many participants were clustered at the bottom of the scale—and how few at the top.

◆ *Leaking Like a Sieve:* productivity is poor; nonprofit is likely to be losing money; growth is difficult.

◆ *Call the Productivity Helpline:* productivity needs serious attention; nonprofit is struggling to stay in place; growth is possible but at high cost.

◆ *Time for Preventive Productivity Maintenance:* productivity is moderate; nonprofit risks losing ground; growth is manageable with effort.

◆ *Watertight:* highest levels of productivity; nonprofit is doing very well; growth is sustainable; capacity-building is manageable; innovation and continuous improvement are a way of life.

More than half the nonprofits surveyed came in at the lowest or second-to-lowest levels of productivity. Fully 79 percent of agencies completing the assessment rated themselves as having failed to embrace some of the nine best practices or having embraced them at a level that leaves considerable room for improvement. A mere 2 percent scored at the Watertight level!

The Context for Productivity

Productive, effective fundraising is a result of many different factors, but one of the most pertinent is the cost of time. Time is a finite resource, and once it's gone, it's gone. Many nonprofit organizations have very small development shops or none at all, which means that those who do the actual work of fundraising have many other demands on their time. Failing to hire development staff because "we can't afford it" may be a false economy.

So we approached the Leaky Bucket study assuming that fundraising time is scarce and precious. Calculations performed with our clients show that once

> What do the Leaky Bucket study results mean? They mean that too many nonprofits are working harder than they need to, to get results that are adequate are at best, and difficult to sustain.
>
> **watch out!**

you take away all the time you have to devote to nonfundraising activities, there are only a limited number of hours left over for raising money. So those hours should produce a fairly large amount of income. Think of this as a "return on effort" calculation. For every hour you invest in cultivating donors or doing other fundraising work, you want to produce lots of money. The range goes from about $1,000 to more than $18,000 per hour. No, that doesn't mean they're not paying you enough! That would be the subject of another book. It just means that you should get a lot of money in return for your investment of time and effort—and you really don't have that much time to begin with.

How to Calculate Your Opportunity Risk Factor	
Total number of days in a year	365
Minus weekend days	104
Minus holidays	
Minus vacation days	
Minus sick days	
Minus days devoted to travel	
Minus days devoted to administration (writing reports, etc.)	
Minus days devoted to giving programs or services	
Total number of days left	
Multiply number of days by eight (eight hours in a day)	
Enter your income target (amount of money you need to raise)	
Divide your income target by your number of hours	
Your opportunity risk factor	

You can find a link to the Opportunity Risk Calculator in **Appendix A.**

Let's explore the nine Leaky Bucket study results now.

Statement #1: Choose Your Nonprofit's Standard Practices for Qualifying Prospective Funders.

The first statement measures whether you have a documented set of criteria for qualifying donor prospects. Here are the choices. The graph shows the distribution of answers.

❑ No standards; we just go after what looks good.

❑ Preferences but no documented standards; we go after funders and donors whose granting guidelines match our needs.

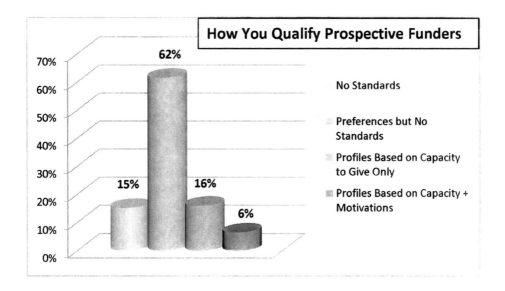

We have profiles for each funding category based on the donor/funder's capacity to give, grant guidelines, or giving history.

We have documented profiles for each funding category; they include donor motivation and preferences as well as the standard wealth profile.

To our dismay, about 76 percent of those who completed the study reported either *no* standards for selecting funding prospects or "preferences" but no documented standards.

It appears that many development hours are thrown away in the process of cultivating funders who are DOA—dead on arrival—from the outset. In other words, development officers are calling on, or attempting to build relationships with, funding prospects based on no meaningful evidence other than "gut feel" or intuition. Prospecting efforts based on such subjective criteria cost time and money but don't necessarily pay off in better prospects. Think about it this way. If your opportunity risk factor is a thousand dollars an hour, then it costs you about a thousand bucks to take a prospect to lunch, *not* including the cost of the lunch. Shouldn't you know as early as possible whether you're going to get a return on your investment?

Best Practices for Qualifying Donor Prospects

If you put together a set of criteria describing your ideal donor, grantor, or corporate giver, you'll save a huge amount of time that you might otherwise waste chasing prospects that don't have the money or the motivation to support you. That's time you can't get back. To avoid this level of waste, document your selection criteria.

◆ Write down the characteristics of your "ideal" funder. Start with the standard criteria, such as age, gender, address, giving history, net worth, etc.

◆ Include motivations for giving, not just wealth profile and giving history. Figure out why your best donors give to you today and use that information in your profile.

◆ Use your qualifying criteria early in the relationship to figure out how much time and energy the prospect justifies.

◆ Stop attempting to cultivate funding prospects that offer little value in return for your efforts.

Base your criteria on your best or favorite current funders. Those are the funders you want to clone. If you don't have funders in a particular category yet, make an educated guess, and then refine your guesses from experience.

Don't put a lot of time and effort into cultivating prospects that don't fit your criteria. It takes real discipline to ignore or put less time into the ones that don't. The temptation is strong to continue pursuing them. But try to resist; you're just throwing away your time if you chase them.

Statement #2. Choose Your Agency's Standard Practices for Acquiring New Funding Sources.

For the last few years, there's been a lot of emphasis on donor retention. But no matter how many donors you retain, you'll always need to acquire new ones as well. If you concentrate only on retention, your donor base will gradually shrink. But as this graph shows, only a small portion of participants are paying enough attention to acquisition.

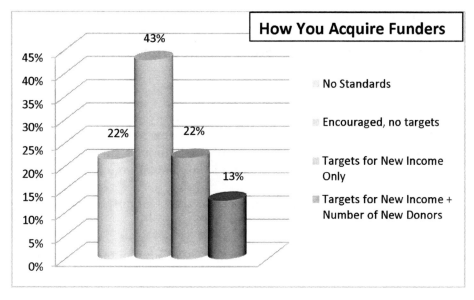

□ No standard practices or targets; we just try as hard as we can every year.

□ We encourage acquiring new funders but don't set specific targets.

□ We set targets for acquiring new-donor gifts and grants, based on income only.

□ We set targets for number of new donors per funding category as well as amount of dollars raised from new sources.

Responses to this statement showed that a staggering 65 percent of respondents lack documented criteria for selecting the funding prospects that justify further effort. Without such standards, therefore, they rely on intuition, past experience, and so on. What's the risk? You could easily put too much time into the wrong prospects, leaving you little time to cultivate the right ones. Even when you do a great job at donor retention, if you don't also concentrate on bringing in new donors, you'll end up in the soup.

You always need new donors. There is attrition; donors die, after all, and they don't always leave their money to you! Furthermore, it's really tough to grow your overall income if you don't bring in new money from new sources, even though the cost of acquiring a new donor is at least six times that of retaining a current one.

What you measure is what you get, and what you don't measure, you *don't* get. So if you fail to issue specific targets for new-funder income and for numbers of new funders per category, you end up undercutting your own efforts.

Best Practices for Qualifying and Acquiring New Funding Sources

Decide on two targets: how much income from new sources, and how many new sources. If you concentrate only on amount of income, you might try to skate by with one or two huge hits, leaving yourself vulnerable.

◆ Establish and document specific targets for number of new funding sources acquired per category.

◆ Establish and document specific targets for amount of money from new funding sources.

◆ Evaluate performance against plan often, at least once a month.

Statement #3: Choose Your Agency's Standard Practices for Retaining Current Donors.

Donor retention is a hugely important issue. AFP even has a special project called the Fundraising Effectiveness Project (FEP) focused on retention. It takes a lot less money and effort to keep a funding source than it does to acquire a new one.

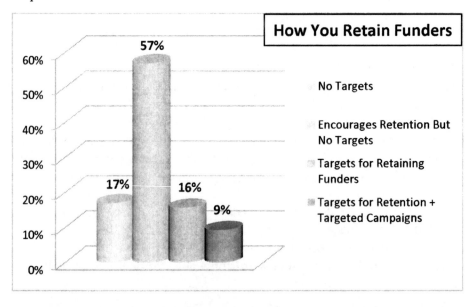

❑ Our agency has no standard practices or targets for retaining donors or renewing grants.

❑ Our agency encourages donor retention but does not assign specific targets for doing so.

❑ Our agency sets specific performance targets for retaining donors.

❑ Our agency has standard, documented practices for retaining current donors that include total dollars raised from current donors and number of donors retained from prior years.

Donor retention is a critically important function, considering the cost of acquiring new funders (six times more costly!). Retaining donors also gives you many more opportunities to upgrade them and strengthen your relationship with them. But the Leaky Bucket study tells us that almost three-quarters of respondents, a total of 73 percent, admitted to having no retention targets or practices, or claimed to have undocumented "preferences" for retention.

Failing to pay attention to the specifics of donor retention is a surefire way to waste scarce and precious fundraising time. It's also a great way to annoy your current donors and leave them with the impression that they'll hear from you only when you want to pester them for more money.

Best Practices for Donor Retention

Think about this issue and make sure you measure your donor-retention performance at regular intervals throughout the year. It's a lot easier to fix your retention practices before they go completely off the rails.

◆ Establish and document donor-retention targets.

◆ Distribute or publish such targets, and make sure that everybody knows about them. Don't assume that people will remember them.

◆ Review actual donor-retention performance against planned donor-retention performance at least once a month. Once a year isn't often enough.

Statement #4. Choose Your Agency's Standard Practices for Upgrading ("Up-Selling" And "Cross-Selling") Your Current Funders.

It's clear that donor retention is important. But are you taking advantage of opportunities to persuade your funders to give larger gifts? (That's up-selling.) Or to underwrite more than one project or campaign at a time? (That's cross-selling.) P.S., upgrading current funders is part and parcel of stewardship.

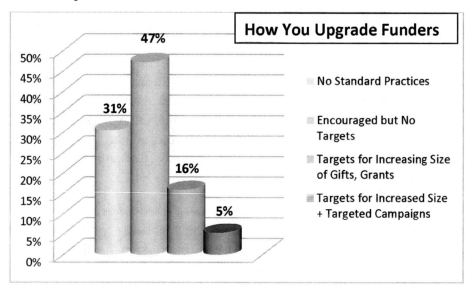

☐ Our agency has no standard practices; we just try hard every year.

☐ Our agency encourages development of current donors but doesn't assign any specific targets or run any fundraising programs to do so.

☐ We set targets every year for increasing the size of gifts, extension of grants, etc.

☐ We set specific targets and goals for up-selling and cross-selling major donors, corporate partners, and grantors, with specific campaigns for doing so.

Up-selling and cross-selling are terms common to the world of corporate sales. Up-selling means convincing the client to buy more than originally discussed. Fast-food chains are geniuses at up-selling. Remember the last time somebody said "do you want fries with that?" "Cross-selling" means persuading the customer to buy something related to the purchase. Think about the last time you bought a computer. I bet the cashier told you, "for only XX dollars more, you can buy an extended warranty," or "we have a special price on such-and-such software you could use with your new computer."

In fundraising, we can ask the donor who gave fifty dollars last year to give one hundred dollars this year. We can also ask that same donor to buy a brick in the memorial walk or get involved in a special-purpose campaign.

Scores for Statement #4 were also disappointing, with 30 percent of agencies reporting that they have no such standard practices. Another 47 percent say that up-selling and cross-selling are "encouraged," but no targets are set in the development plan. Only 5 percent set targets and run specific campaigns for up-selling and cross-selling.

Encouraged means "We talk about its importance but don't establish specific management controls and objectives to make sure we *do* it."

Establishing performance metrics for this area of fund development is just as pertinent as any of the other statement areas. Without such metrics, you and your development team are very likely to leave money on the table, as the saying goes. In fact, these practices are intimately tied to donor retention.

Best Practices for Upgrading Retained Funders

Set and document specific targets for upgrading your funders. That way, you'll be able to evaluate progress against plan and keep the team focused on these desirable, productive practices.

◆ Establish and document targets for up-selling (raising the size of gifts or grants) and cross-selling (getting funders to underwrite new or different projects while still giving to their current ones).

◆ Prepare specific marketing campaigns for up-sell/cross-sell purposes.

◆ Establish strategic development plans every year with each major donor or other major funder. In the for-profit world, these are called "account plans." That might be a good practice to adopt in the third sector!

◆ Conduct annual or biannual reviews with each of these major funding sources.

Statement #5. Choose Your Agency's Standard Practices for Funding Diversification.

Diversifying your sources of income is clearly a desirable practice, and we were happy to see a large percentage of participants show that they pay attention to it. We can't overemphasize the importance of diversifying your funding sources. This is especially important for many US-based social service agencies that have traditionally been funded primarily (or entirely) by only one or a few renewable grants from county, state, or federal

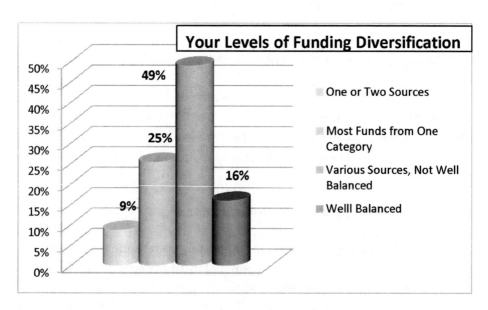

agencies. Once that funding source is reduced or eliminated, the nonprofit can run into huge difficulties.

- ❑ Most of our funding comes from a small number of sources, especially state or local agencies. We don't think about funding diversification very much.

- ❑ Most of our funding comes from one category, like grants. We only have a few other types of funders (corporate sponsors, individual donors) and need to work on this.

- ❑ We get funding from a variety of sources, although the level of funding diversity is still not balanced well.

- ❑ Our funding is well balanced among a variety of funding sources, with no single funder accounting for more than a defined proportion of total income.

Happily, 49 percent report that they are at the third-highest level of productivity in terms of funding diversification, and another healthy minority, 16 percent, has reached the "well-balanced" level. But we still see about 9 percent of all nonprofits having few funders (or only one), while another 25 percent rely on funders in a single category, such as grants.

> You may only be able to change proportions of diversification by as little as 10 percent a year, so start diversifying early, before you lose one of those key funders.

By definition, nonprofits that rank low on this particular scale are extremely vulnerable. If just one of their funders withdraws, the agency could fail.

Best Practices for Funding Diversification

No matter if your levels of diversification are well balanced, or not so well, this is an area of fund development that deserves constant thought.

- ◆ Document specific growth targets for each funding category, where the target is a percentage or proportion of total income.

◆ Document specific retention targets for each funding category, including retention of amount of money as well as number of funders in each category.

◆ Review actual diversification performance and compare with planned diversification performance at least once a month.

Statement #6: Choose Your Agency's Standard Practices Regarding Staff Resources for Fundraising.

Staffing has an enormous impact on fundraising productivity. Agencies that avoid hiring development professionals may be making a very costly mistake. And this holds true for established organizations as well as those that are start-ups or small grassroots outfits.

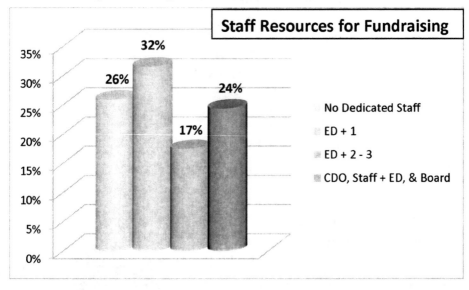

❑ We have no fundraising staff; our executive director does all the fundraising, operational, and program work.

❑ We have at least one fundraising staff person full time or part time in addition to the executive director.

❑ We have two or more staff members who do fundraising work as well as support tasks.

❑ We have a development director plus staff dedicated to fundraising. We also get our board and senior leadership involved.

This is a tricky area to figure out. Smaller agencies tend to have smaller development staffs, often none, relying on the executive director to do all the fundraising work, which is something we expected to see. But here's the problem—fundraising is a full-time job. In fact, when we calculate the opportunity risk factor for executive directors with no development staff, their risk factors come in at significantly higher levels, often as much as $3,000 an hour.

Nonprofit CEOs have to make a decision that can be problematic for any entrepreneur: What is my job? If it's programs, then time spent on development compromises programs. If it's development, then time spent on programs compromises development. And if the executive director's job is one of executive leadership and management, then the work of programs and of development must be someone else's job. The answer to this problem is to recognize the strategic importance of the development function and to hire development personnel as early as possible in the agency's evolution. Staff dedicated to fundraising is as important as staff dedicated to programs or client service.

Best Practices for Development Staff Resources

Hiring your first development professional might be just as important (sometimes more) as hiring your first program or clinical manager.

- ◆ Avoid "work until you drop" heroism. Executive directors who work ninety-plus hours a week are going to burn out and do substandard work. Or quit.

- ◆ Understand the strategic importance of development; don't allow your senior executives or board to downplay it.

Moving development out of the shadows includes paying staff a competitive wage and giving the development person a title equal to that of similar positions in your organization. For example, if you have a vice president for finance and a vice president of operations, your development person should be vice president of development, not director of development. Development staff is just as important as your technical, clinical, or program staff; hire development personnel as soon as you can possibly justify it.

 practical tip

◆ Move development "out of the shadows"; help staff and board understand how much it costs to achieve your mission.

◆ If you can't afford development staff, adjust your performance targets and expectations downward.

◆ Build your case for hiring development staff by facts, not passion.

Statement #7. How Does Your Agency Measure Fundraising Performance Today? Check All That Apply.

We were surprised by the responses to this statement. After all, we thought, so many agencies already report on outcomes, achievements, and other metrics demanded by their grantors and other funders; surely they also use good metrics for development. But fundraising metrics are another story.

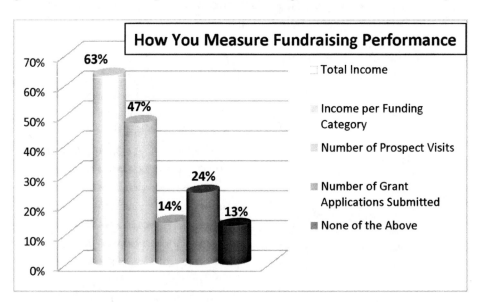

❑ Overall income compared with our fundraising goal

❑ Income for each funding category compared with our goal for that category

❑ Number of times we visit with major donors, corporate sponsors, etc.

❑ Number of grant applications or donor proposals we produce

❑ None of the above

The results of this particular statement were truly sobering. First, we expected and, in fact, wanted to see *everybody* using income and income per category as key indicators. But we see that only 63 percent of respondents keep track of total income and 47 percent keep track of income by category, when both categories should be close to 100 percent. How come? Does this suggest that there are nonprofits out there whose funding goal is simply "Bring in as much as we can, and then we'll figure out how to spend it"? Just thinking about what that means makes us nervous!

Next sobering thought: Income and income by category are trailing indicators. Although they are vitally important, they are weak at telling you how efficient or productive you were in reaching the targets. We offered a couple of leading indicators that would complement the trailers, namely visits with donors and number of applications produced. As you see, only a minority of respondents chose those options. Fourteen percent chose "visits with donors," and 24 percent measured number of grant applications or proposals. A depressing 13 percent said "none of the above," which means they are not measuring anything—or they are measuring something we never thought of.

Best Practices for Measuring Fundraising Performance

Many of our clients and colleagues have confessed that they don't know "where to start" when it comes to metrics and measurements. Try to work with simple things like these first. You can choose others as you become more experienced.

◆ *Always* set targets for overall income and for each funding category. Failing to establish such targets actually slows down the fundraising process.

◆ Set other leading indicators as well, such as number of times in a month you qualify prospects or number of times prospects indicate their willingness to accept a proposal from you.

◆ Set targets for the entire year and for monthly intervals. If more money comes in at certain times of the year, make sure your targets reflect such seasonality.

Statement #8. Does Your Agency Have a Comprehensive Fundraising Tool Kit? Check All Items That Your Agency Actually Uses on a Regular Basis.

The fundraising tool kit is sometimes called the fundraising infrastructure. If you haven't put the basics in place, then doing the ongoing day-to-day work will be more difficult—and considerably more time-consuming.

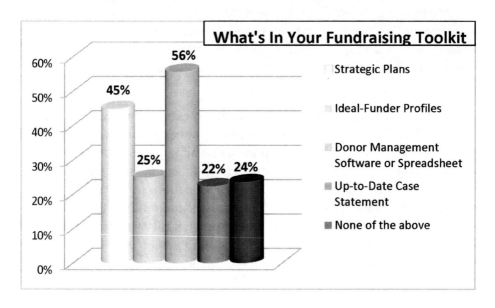

What's In Your Fundraising Toolkit

- Strategic Plans
- Ideal-Funder Profiles
- Donor Management Software or Spreadsheet
- Up-to-Date Case Statement
- None of the above

- ❑ Strategic development plan with specific fundraising goals and objectives

- ❑ Prospect profiles for qualifying donors, grantors, corporate sponsors

- ❑ Donor management software

- ❑ Formal case statement

- ❑ None of the above

This statement produced a mixed response. Use of donor-management software scored highest; 56 percent said they have a software application or use a

Put together a good fundraising tool kit. Without it, your fundraising people will waste time that you can't afford to lose and can't replace.

practical tip

spreadsheet, and about 45 percent said they have a strategic development plan. On the other hand, relatively few reported having a formal and up-to-date case statement (only 22 percent), and only 25 percent reported having donor/prospect profiles.

This finding is meaningful. If your fundraising tool kit lacks ideal-funder or prospect profiles, a strategic development plan with funding goals, or a way to centralize all information about donors and donor prospects, you are making it very tough for fundraising to succeed. Good materials, preparation, and metrics will make your team efficient and productive.

Best Practices for Creating a Fundraising Tool Kit

Put the kit together before you start fundraising activities. If you don't put the pieces in place, then you have to reinvent them every time you need them. And that means burning up even more time that you can't afford or replace.

- ◆ Start with the fundraising "game plan" (development plan), a document containing qualifying criteria for selecting funding prospects, income targets, targets for retention, new-donor acquisition, and any/all policies related to fundraising (see **Chapter Two**).

- ◆ Then add materials that you can share with or show to prospects, including the up-to-date case statement, presentation templates, annual report or fundraising brochures, and a list of suggested probing questions to ask prospects.

Statement #9. Check the Following Techniques Your Nonprofit Uses When Fundraising Performance Runs Below Desired Levels. Choose As Many As You Wish.

If your fundraising results are less than desirable, then you'll want to do something to make them better. Or so we hope and trust. If you have systematic methods for improving those undesirable results, your fundraising will improve. If you're simply shooting from the hip, then improvement is a matter of chance.

❑ Fire our development director.

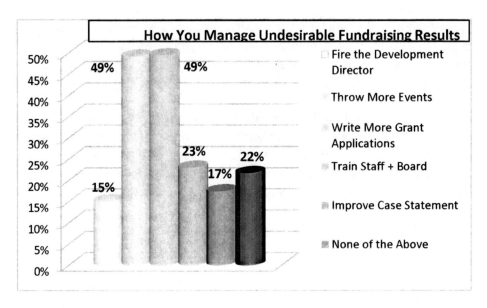

How You Manage Undesirable Fundraising Results

- 49% Throw More Events
- 49% Write More Grant Applications
- 23% Train Staff + Board
- 17% Improve Case Statement
- 22% None of the Above
- 15% Fire the Development Director

Legend:
- Fire the Development Director
- Throw More Events
- Write More Grant Applications
- Train Staff + Board
- Improve Case Statement
- None of the Above

- ❑ Increase number of fundraising activities or events.

- ❑ Write more grant applications.

- ❑ Provide staff/board solicitor training.

- ❑ Improve, update our case statement.

- ❑ None of the above.

Based on our survey responses, there is a trend toward using high-cost, low-return methods for managing undesirable performance. The most popular choice is increasing the number of fundraising events, at 49 percent. Unfortunately this is often a bad idea, or at least an expensive one. Yet it's often the first suggestion that surfaces when fundraising performance runs below desired levels. And since your board probably proposed this event frenzy, it's tough to say no. Preparing more grant applications and donor proposals got the same score, 49 percent. Although there is a correlation between level of activity and level of results, who's to say that simply putting out more applications will get you where you want to go?

One of the two moderate-cost, higher-return options was staff/board solicitor training. This option was chosen by about 23 percent of the survey. Training can be a great investment with benefits that continue to accrue over the long term.

The lowest score we got was for improving the case statement. Only 17 percent of respondents said that they used this option when fundraising was down. Improving the case statement is simple enough to do, and it's quite inexpensive too, considering that you can usually improve it using in-house resources.

We were pleased to see that only 15 percent of respondents chose "Fire the development director." Although it's sometimes necessary to do so, it can be extremely costly to find, replace, and train the replacement. You'll get in trouble only if firing the development director is your standard "fix" for improving fundraising results.

Best Practices for Managing Undesirable Fundraising Results

If you've got to reinvent the wheel every time fundraising results fall below desired levels, you are wasting a great chance to improve productivity. Put practices like these into place today.

◆ Analyze your performance metrics month after month to monitor your trends.

◆ Avoid knee-jerk reactions if performance falls below desired levels.

◆ Fundraising events are expensive and risky; consider the cost/ benefit ratio of using them.

◆ Expand and upgrade your performance metrics, benchmarks, and guidelines

To Recap

◆ Fundraising time is scarce, precious, and irreplaceable. Understand its value and invest it wisely.

◆ Make sure you support your fundraising efforts with documented qualifying criteria, performance metrics, and success targets.

◆ Document these criteria and performance indicators. Don't assume that people will remember them.

◆ Only 2 percent of all nonprofits studied to date rate their fundraising productivity at the "watertight" level. Let's raise that percentage!

Chapter Two

Evaluating Your Fundraising Infrastructure

IN THIS CHAPTER

···➤ Your fundraising goals and objectives—do they support the goals of your strategic plan?

···➤ Do you have the infrastructure in place to support your fundraising activities—policies, procedures, donor software?

···➤ What do you need to put into place to strengthen your infrastructure?

The Leaky Bucket study suggests that good infrastructure is both critical and conspicuous by its absence. This chapter addresses the fundraising infrastructure by reviewing its major components and offering suggestions on how to implement them.

What's wrong with the planning that we see today? Let us count the ways:

◆ There is no strategic plan, or it's not documented. ("We already know what we're going to do.")

◆ There is a plan, but it's too high-level to guide the actions of anybody.

◆ There is a plan that somebody or other put together some time back in the past; whatever happened to that plan, anyway?

◆ There's a great, dandy, sophisticated plan just chock full of guidelines and metrics and instructions, but we look at it only when it's time to create a new plan.

Failing to plan means planning to fail.

important

It is critical that you have a well-designed, documented strategic plan in place that expresses your organization's goals and objectives for the next one to three years. The high-level goals of the strategic plan are then supported by the development plan. In other words, the goals and objectives of the development plan must make it possible for the strategic goals and objectives to be achieved. Every organization needs to have a strategic plan and a development plan. Sometimes the strategic plan is called the long-range plan.

Typically a nonprofit will have a strategic plan with a healthy timeline (three years is typical). The strategic plan is the overall road map to take an organization where its leadership wants it to go. Within the strategic plan, you should have a development plan, a program plan, a financial plan, and a facilities plan. For the purposes of this book, we focus on the development plan and how it supports the strategic plan, but you should have a good understanding of your organization's strategic plan as well.

Some nonprofits call their strategic plan a business plan, especially if they have had influence from board members or funders who are businesspeople. However, a business plan is a different animal, since its purpose is to clarify the amount of money needed to operate the business (for-profit or nonprofit) at a certain level of capacity. Typically business plans are submitted to funding institutions (banks, venture-capital companies, foundations, wealthy investors, or donors); such plans are designed to sell the concept of the business to your potential underwriters and show the prospective funder that you know how to run the enterprise.

definition

Questions You Should Ask Yourself about Your Strategic Plan

Whether you have a strategic plan, or you're just getting ready to produce one, make sure you have asked and answered questions like these. If not, then it might be a plan, but it won't be strategic.

◆ Does our strategic plan encompass all the supplemental plans, such as the development plan, that we need to reach our vision and fulfill our mission?

◆ Did we have input from all the necessary people in developing our strategic plan: board, staff, clients, funders, our community?

◆ Did we use an outside facilitator to ensure that the process stayed on track and that we utilized the input received from all of our stakeholders?

◆ Does our plan have realistic but visionary goals?

◆ Does our plan have SMART objectives?

◆ Does our plan include the strategies to implement our objectives?

◆ Have we assigned timelines, areas of responsibility, and budgets to all the action steps in our plan to ensure that it gets implemented?

◆ Is every objective assigned to a staff member *by name* who is then held accountable for results?

◆ Is our development plan aligned with the strategic plan, and is it also aligned "horizontally," to avoid misalignment with other operating units within the organization?

◆ Does the plan include clear, specific ways to measure success and performance targets for every objective?

◆ Did we set up the plan with annual and monthly targets, so we can review progress against plan at least once a month?

◆ Do we review progress against plan religiously, at least once a month?

Once you have a solid strategic plan in place, you can begin to create your development plan. The development plan answers the questions: "What should it cost to achieve our mission? How are we going to get there? How do we raise the money to realize our vision? How do we measure success?"

Like the strategic plan, the development plan must have broad-based goals, SMART objectives, strategies, and action steps that answer these questions:

> **SMART Objectives**
>
> SMART objectives are:
>
> ◆ **S**pecific
>
> ◆ **M**easurable
>
> ◆ **A**ction oriented
>
> ◆ **R**ealistic
>
> ◆ **T**ime defined

◆ Who is going to be held accountable for the results of this objective? Who is going to be the "owner"—that is, the person who holds others accountable?

◆ How much is it going to cost and/or how much is it going to raise?

◆ Are all the necessary tools, resources, or information needed to do the job properly available at this time, or do you have to create/purchase them?

◆ When is the action step going to be completed?

Also, just like the strategic plan, your development plan should start with a current assessment of your fundraising situation. You should do a SWOT analysis of your development program, just as you would do an analysis of your entire organization during the strategic planning process. While there are numerous ways to measure your development program, the SWOT analysis is one tool that can help you assess your performance. This book will take you through a step-by-step analysis program. Keep in mind that the many things you are doing right (strengths) will help you deal with the things that are "wrong" with your development program (weaknesses). Looking at opportunities and threats (the external or marketplace factors that can affect your development success) will also help you use these assessment tools in your own unique situation.

When conducting your SWOT analysis, consider your strengths from an outsider's perspective. What strengths does your organization appear to have, in the eyes of your clients, funders, board members, community in general? Asking these questions helps you stay away from listing soft abstractions such as "teamwork" and "great people."

Your SWOT Analysis Measures

◆ Internal **S**trengths

◆ Internal **W**eaknesses

◆ External **O**pportunities

◆ External **T**hreats

Similar to the questions you've asked yourself about your strategic planning process, you should also look at your development process and ask:

◆ Did you get input from all the right people: development staff, CEO, board, volunteers, and donors?

◆ Do you have visionary goals and SMART objectives?

◆ Are your goals and objectives reasonable, yet still motivating?

◆ Is your development plan aligned with your strategic plan?

◆ Did you assign areas of responsibility, timelines, and budgets for each action step?

◆ Do you have metrics and benchmarks that drive execution, predictability, and consistency?

If your planning process and/or product are not all they should be, what are some of the ways you could strengthen the process and/or the product?

❑ We need to develop a strategic plan or update the one we currently have.

❑ We need to engage an outside facilitator to help us with the strategic planning process.

❑ We need to take our current strategic plan and assign areas of accountability, budgets, and timelines to each action step.

❑ We need to create a development plan or update the one we currently have.

❑ We need to do a thorough assessment of our development program.

❑ We need to assign areas of responsibility, timelines, and budgets to our development action steps.

Policies and Procedures

We could relate dozens of stories about organizations that suffered because they did not have policies and procedures in place before they started fundraising. Policies are critical for several reasons:

◆ Staff should not need to reinvent the wheel every time a unique gift or situation comes along.

◆ Donors have the right to know that their gifts are being used the way they wanted them to be used and that you are acting in a professional manner according to the highest ethical and legal standards.

◆ Documented policies tend to prevent making the same mistakes over and over again.

◆ Volunteers who will help with fundraising should never be put into a position where they are not sure what type of gifts you will accept, from whom you will or will not accept gifts, and how you will use or dispose of those gifts.

Policies should be developed by staff, approved by the board, and made available to everyone who is involved in fundraising for your organization. Once they have been published initially, they should remain easily accessible in your information systems so they can be updated as needed.

What Should Be Included in Your Gift Acceptance Policies?

Gift acceptance policies help protect you from situations such as accepting a gift of land only to find that it needs major soil remediation, or a gift of a building filled with asbestos. Or from accepting a gift from a convicted felon, or one with strings attached to it that are not in the best interest of your organization. Some things you should include in your gift acceptance polices are:

♦ from whom you will/will not accept gifts;

♦ types of gifts you will/ will not accept;

♦ gift conditions you will/ will not accept;

♦ due diligence process for determining gift acceptance;

♦ a process for making exceptions to policies; and

♦ how you will dispose of gifts that you cannot use.

> **Policies You Need to Have in Place**
>
> ❑ Gift acceptance policies
>
> ❑ Recognition policies
>
> ❑ Investment policies
>
> ❑ Policies regarding how to prepare for and conduct a meeting with a donor prospect, especially when a volunteer or board member is involved in the meeting

important

Questions That Should Be Answered by Your Recognition Policies

You will also want to have policies for how you recognize donors. Some questions to be considered when developing recognition policies include:

♦ At what level of giving will you consider naming a building, area, or program in honor or memory of a donor?

♦ What type of recognition events or items will you provide for donors?

♦ What tax considerations will impact recognition items given to donors?

♦ How do we ensure the ability of donors to remain anonymous if they choose to do so?

What Should Be Included in Your Investment Policies?

You should also have policies to determine how you will invest gifts of cash or stock.

Investing the money once you raise it is important too. Ask yourself:

◆ how aggressive/conservative your investment policy will be;

◆ what you will do with gifts of stock your organization might consider to be "socially unacceptable;" and

◆ who will make the decision as to who will manage your investments.

A conflict-of-interest policy should be created to ensure that the people making investment decisions are not directly benefiting from those decisions.

Policies for Preparing for and Managing Visits with Donor Prospects

Of course, first you have to raise the money before you can invest it, recognize it, and make sure it is something you want to accept. To get ready to make the ask, start here:

◆ What you will need to know about the prospect in order to determine which staff members and/or board members should participate in the visit.

◆ How you will prepare any volunteers or board members for their roles in the visit.

◆ What you will need to have prepared ahead of time, such as formal case statement, collateral or leave-behind documents, development targets, copy of ideal-funder profile, suggested questions to ask the prospect.

◆ What you and any volunteers involved agree to be your goal for the visit.

◆ What you and any volunteers involved agree to be the appropriate follow-up actions after the visit.

Office Procedures

You will also need basic procedures in place for things such as:

◆ Who receives the donations and opens the mail?

◆ Who records the gift in the database and sends the thank-you letters?

◆ How quickly does a gift get acknowledged?

◆ Who signs the acknowledgment letters?

◆ At what point do donors receive a form letter, a handwritten note, and/or a phone call to thank them for their donation?

◆ When is the official IRS letter sent to donors?

◆ Who deposits the checks?

◆ How are gifts recorded in your database system, and how is that information transferred to the finance department?

Written procedures are important because there will be occasions when the person responsible for one of these duties is unavailable and someone else needs to take over that person's job for a day, a week, or even longer. Donor stewardship is critical to fundraising, and without written procedures, things such as recording, reporting, and acknowledging gifts might fall through the cracks. These procedures are developed by staff and do not need board approval.

> A good procedure is to thank donors within twenty-four hours of the receipt of their gift.

practical
tip

What Do You Need to Develop?

So, let's analyze what you need to develop in the way of policies and procedures.

We need to:

- ❑ Develop gift acceptance policies, **OR**
- ❑ Review and possibly revise our gift acceptance policies.

- ❑ Develop recognition policies, **OR**
- ❑ Review and possibly revise our recognition policies.

- ❑ Develop investment policies, **OR**
- ❑ Review and possibly revise our investment policies.

- ❑ Have the board approve our policies.

- ❑ Make our policies known to anyone who is involved in fundraising for our organization.

- ❑ Develop written procedures for the recording, reporting, and acknowledgment of donations, or

- ❑ Review and possibly revise our written procedures for recording, reporting, and acknowledging donations.

- ❑ Ensure that anyone responsible for any aspect of this process is aware of our procedures and is following them.

You'll find suggestions for fundraising policies at a number of sites. Some of the best and most complete include:

- ❑ The Foundation Center

- ❑ The Grantsmanship Center

- ❑ Fundsvcs.org

- ❑ AFPnet.org

To Recap

- ◆ The infrastructure of your nonprofit enterprise rests on a foundation of planning, policy, and procedure. If the plans are naïve, inconsistent, or out of date, or if they fail to drive desirable levels of execution, your nonprofit's foundation will be shaky. And it's a lot tougher to fix the foundation after the building is built than it is if you set it up the right way in the first place.

◆ The policies that you develop are also fundamental to the integrity and performance of your nonprofit organization. Never assume that everybody "already knows" what is expected of them; you are bound to discover that their understanding is varied at best, unless you and your leadership commit to clarifying expectations and guidelines. This is one of those situations where an ounce of prevention is worth a pound of cure.

Chapter Three

Technology: The Glue That Holds It All Together

IN THIS CHAPTER

···➔ What's wrong with your technology anyway?

···➔ Understanding the three categories of technology that you absolutely, positively must have

···➔ Making technology work for you, and not the other way around

What's wrong with nonprofit technology anyway? Well, from the perspective of those who create and sell nonprofit technology, nothing. But if you're looking at the way nonprofit organizations *use* technology, let's just say there's room for improvement. For example, the Leaky Bucket study shows us that only 56 percent of respondents have any sort of donor-management software, even a simple spreadsheet. In this day and age, failing to adopt basic technology for such a critical function is pretty hard to fathom.

It's all too common to find businesses of all types, nonprofit and for-profit alike, that don't have a clear understanding of their information or communication needs. Yet they invest in or accept donations of technology that may or may not suit their needs, budgets, or capacity for using it.

In this chapter, we concentrate on helping you figure out what you need in the way of technology so that you can either fix the gaps in what you currently own or invest in new technology that will get the job done right.

Most of all, we would like to see you avoid some common technology errors, such as these:

◆ Information about donors and prospects is all over the place, kept in a variety of systems and formats, so it's tough to collate or make sense of it.

◆ The website is out of date, information on it is static, visitors can't interact with it, and nobody on your staff can fix or make changes to it because you have to wait for "the website guy" to do it for you.

◆ Mechanisms for marketing and outreach are clumsy, used inconsistently, or require special skills that you don't have and can't afford.

◆ The tools you use to keep track of money are out of sync with the tools you use to keep track of donors.

◆ You don't allocate enough money to maintain current technology or take advantage of new, more effective technology tools.

◆ You are (blissfully?) ignorant of the many services and resources that provide technology tools to nonprofit organizations for free or at greatly reduced prices.

◆ When planning a technology investment, you overlook the true cost of ownership in favor of a low cost of entry.

Let's fix this now.

The Three Types of Technology You Absolutely, Positively Have to Have

Every nonprofit organization, regardless of size or mission, embraces three critical business functions that require the use of good information technology:

◆ How you cultivate, attract, retain, and manage relationships with funders, clients, and other constituents;

◆ How you communicate with funders, prospects, volunteers, clients, staff, board, and others; and

◆ How you manage the money.

Although there are meaningful overlaps among these functions, they each require fundamentally different solutions. Before you give any thought at all to which vendor or format or nifty-cool application that you heard about from your buddy, think through what you need to do to handle these three mission-critical functions.

Managing Relationships with Funders, Clients, and Others

Your nonprofit comes into the world with quite a range of constituencies: individuals, groups, and other organizations that have some vested interest in your nonprofit and mission. In terms of fundraising, there are two primary constituencies: current donors and prospective donors (and that includes grantors and corporate donors). Other constituents include clients, staff, board, volunteers, vendors, advisors, and key community influencers. You need to manage relationships with all these constituencies. Managing these relationships runs from simply being able to phone them or schedule a lunch date to running a fundraising campaign and keeping track of their responses. A generic name for the software applications that address this range of functions is "CRM," or constituent relationship management.

> This chapter talks about information needs, not about the products that could satisfy those needs. You'll find references to various resources and vendor sites in **Appendix A**, but first figure out what you want to do!

important

A CRM system is a dynamic database. That means it is a repository of information about all the contacts you have or want to have. It includes both static and dynamic (changing) information. Static information changes rarely (name, company, title, address, phone number, etc.), while dynamic information may change frequently (type and size of gift, inclusion on the newsletter subscription list, preference for Campaign A over Campaign B, acceptance/rejection of an invitation, date of a planned appointment, etc.) A CRM system is the heart of a successful development office. The information contained in the database will be used for many purposes and must be available in a format that allows easy updating, access, manipulation, reporting, and analysis.

Before we even talk about what the CRM system can do for you, remember that the size of its database is important. It's essential that your database be large enough to satisfy your needs for gift income, volunteer activity, and community influence. P.S., bigger is better. It must also be as up to date as possible, since people change their addresses, phone numbers, even their names. And it must be full of contacts that have a reasonable level of interest in your organization.

This means that you must pay attention to increasing the size of your list or "following," maintaining the accuracy of the list, and capturing information that demonstrates the level of interest and commitment shown by the contacts in the system.

What Can Your CRM System Do for You?

The CRM system is much more than a list. It allows you to manage the relationships you have, or desire to have, with the individuals on the list. Fairly soon after its "birth," your nonprofit's list of contacts will be too large for you to stay in touch with everybody without automated tools.

Good database technology will simplify a wide range of standard functions and also give you the capability to do some interesting things that you simply could not do manually (or if you could do them, they would take hours and hours, thus costing you money you probably don't have). All of these functions allow you to build the relationships it takes to generate gifts and fund your operation.

> The information in your CRM system is more than just a mailing list. It's one of your agency's most critical, competitive assets.
>
>
> important

Range of CRM System Functions

Most CRM systems provide contact management functions, analytical functions, and opportunity-management functions. We'll describe each one in turn.

The contact management functions include:

- *Contact information*: Keep all the names, titles, company affiliations, phone/fax/mobile numbers, email addresses, Twitter handles, LinkedIn profiles, Facebook pages, and so on, in one place, so you can always find who you're looking for.

- *Calendar capabilities*: Don't rely on your memory. Enter every appointment, phone call, meeting, and so on into your calendar. Automated calendars include alert and reminder functions; these send you a reminder about the appointment ahead of time so you don't forget it and associate the appointment with the contact record so you can remind yourself of when you last met (and what you last spoke about).

- *Other related functions:* These include tasks you are supposed to do (call this donor, post to your blog, run that report, and so on), and other kinds of reminders and alerts.

The analytical functions include methods for identifying groups of like individuals, pulling mailing lists to communicate with like individuals, analyzing the size and shape of your constituent groups, and reporting on the levels of growth, etc., of these same constituencies. They include, but are by no means limited to, the following kinds of functions:

- *Categorization*: Is this contact a current donor, a prospect, a donor that used to give but has not given since 1983? Categorization may also include things like age, gender, zip code ("We're sending out a mailing to these zip codes"), preferences ("Does this donor care more about dogs or more about cats?"), or sources ("Did we get this contact from Campaign A or Campaign B?").

- *Profiling information*: Based on your agency's qualifying criteria, does this contact represent high, moderate, or low potential for giving?

- *Campaign information*: Has this contact responded to this or that campaign? At what level? How often have they given?

◆ *Attendance information:* Have contacts attended/said "no" to an event? Did they give or pledge at the event? Did they show up, did they participate in the walkathon, swing a hammer at the building site, host a cocktail party?

◆ *Volunteer information:* Has the contact ever volunteered for anything at your nonprofit? When, where, what did they do? Are they likely to do it again?

Opportunity management is the third function, and it bestows numerous benefits, including a centralized place to keep track of your pipeline of potential gifts and grants. This function also helps you keep track of your fundraising campaigns, keep you focused and up to date as you cultivate individual opportunities, and provide reports and insights that help you improve the performance of your development efforts. These functions are usually integrated into a CRM system but are sometimes managed by a separate application. Collectively, these functions should be thought of as your fundraising system or platform.

Opportunity management functions include:

◆ *Pipeline statistics:* How many individual opportunities are you tracking per category; what is their forecasted income potential; at what stage is each opportunity?

◆ *Pipeline velocity:* How quickly does the average gift, grant, or corporate donation move through the cultivation process?

◆ *Cultivation:* Depending on the stage that the opportunity has reached, what tactics should you employ to move them to the next stage? When should you recruit your CEO or board chair to participate in the effort?

◆ *Conversion ratios:* How many opportunities are you able to convert to the next opportunity stage? How many forecasted opportunities have "converted" to pledged or collected gifts?

CRM System Benefits

Your CRM system must provide three benefits, or it's not worth much. For one thing, it has to make it easy for you to get in touch with your constituents. It does this for you by centralizing contact information about them, making it easy for you to locate such information, and giving you a thumbnail sketch of your relationship to date so you don't sound like an idiot: "Oh hello, Mrs. Jones, it's been so long since we spoke, how is Mr. Jones?" "Sorry, my dear, you must be confused. We had lunch last week to discuss the new roof project. Mr. Jones died last year, and I'm planning to give you his money." Oops.

Second, the database can handle lots of outbound work for you quickly, efficiently, and at low cost. It can pull together all the contacts who should receive the annual appeal letter, separate out the ones who should get the new planned-giving appeal, push those "save the cats and kittens" letters to the people who like cats and not to the ones who like dogs, and so on.

Finally, your CRM system must be able to report to you so you can report to your CEO and/or board. In other words, you really need to know stuff such as how many names are in your database, how many are prospects versus donors, how many have given in the past twelve months, how many have not given for three years or more, how many upgraded their gifts, how many lapsed donors you had this year, when your pledges are expected to be paid, and so on. These reports are among the most valuable tools you have to assess how well your fundraising efforts are working, where you need to improve, and where you could find opportunities for innovation.

If the CRM system you're working with can't do all three of those functions for you, you're not getting what you need out of it and you should probably think about fixing, replacing, or upgrading it. At the very least, get your vendor to provide some training on how to use the system properly.

Some Caveats about Database Systems

In addition to being able to keep track of enormous numbers of individual records, most CRM system software products can store and keep track of an enormous number of *data fields* as well. That's just dandy. In fact, it's wonderful, but it's also a potential mine field. Just because it's easy to identify lots of types of information, enter it, and keep track of it doesn't mean it's a good idea. Getting and keeping too much information, especially information about unimportant stuff, is as damaging as not getting enough information or getting the wrong stuff.

Before you decide to store any information about your contacts above and beyond the basics, you must ask yourself these questions:

◆ What information are we going to need about each contact beyond name, address, and phone number?

◆ What purpose will this particular piece of information serve?

◆ How will we use this information to either maintain the relationship or enhance it?

◆ If we wanted to create a report based on this information, what would it tell us?

◆ What will tracking this information over time do for us?

Just because you *can* keep track of your donor's favorite colors, shoe size, or hair stylist's pet's name doesn't necessarily mean you should do so.

Who's Going to "Touch" the Database?

The technology for information and communications has evolved at a dizzying pace in the last ten years alone, and it looks like the pace of that change is actually growing faster. Among many other things, this rapid evolution now gives us database technology that's a whole lot smarter and easier to use than the so-called "legacy" systems that came into the market ten or more years ago. These contemporary tools are intended to be used directly by the people who have the relationships with the individuals in the database. They eliminate or at least reduce the need for specially trained staff to handle data input and updating.

If I have to write down the information I want recorded in my database, give it to my database expert, then wait until I'm sure it's been recorded, I've just reduced my productivity (and probably driven my blood pressure through the roof). It's a whole lot simpler and more direct for me to get a calendar reminder on my cell phone, swipe it open with a touch of my finger, and key in a note or two about the conversation. That way, I've shortened the cycle time of updating the record and don't have to worry about the errors that crop up every time another person has to translate my ideas.

The process has become so straightforward and simple that it's far more efficient to equip your development team with such easy-to-use tools. The executive director, chief development officer, and board chair should be able to update their interactions themselves.

So the rule of thumb these days is to find CRM systems that are so straightforward that anyone who "touches" the prospect can easily update the record. And for certain reporting functions, you can set up the reports in such a way that running them requires just the click of a button.

Where Special Skills Are Needed

It does *not* make sense to have a senior executive, or a junior one for that matter, doggedly enter zillions of keystrokes to create a database from scratch. If you have to enter lots of contact names by hand, delegate the work to a lower-paid person, outsource it to a service, or get a college intern or volunteer to do it for nothing. If the contacts are already available in a spreadsheet, on your Facebook page, or in your Outlook files, it should be fairly simple to transfer them to your CRM system. That's also a task for a trained but lower-cost person. You don't need software engineers or database experts for this purpose. You might also want to have a well-trained person or two who understand how to set up the reports you want to use regularly or who can run special reports for unique purposes. Either work with your IT staff or have your CRM system vendor train your employee(s).

> When determining who should be entering data, keep in mind the lost-opportunity costs. If you are the chief development officer, does it make more sense for you to spend your time at the computer or out to lunch with a major donor? Most times, the answer is with the major donor, but sometimes it's "in front of the computer!"

practical tip

Working with Legacy Systems

If your nonprofit has been around for a while, you may already have a large, useful database built on one of the older-generation systems. These systems remain extremely powerful and competent, although they tend to

When importing lists of contacts, make sure you have the right permission to do so. Otherwise you may be in violation of the legislation that protects us from spamming and other unwanted intrusions. Many CRM systems and email marketing services will help you figure out if you're in compliance or not.

important

be more difficult to use and usually require the services of a dedicated staff expert. These systems are often referred to as legacy systems because they contain such a vast legacy of critical information that it makes more sense to learn how to use them well than it does to replace them just for the sake of change.

Make sure, however, that you have a highly skilled, trained support person to manage the "care and feeding" of the legacy system and to keep track of the various codes and so on that are used to identify constituent groups. Also make sure that you have documented all the policies and procedures to be used by the development team when it provides information to the staff expert or ask for information or reports back. Standardizing these functions will improve efficiency.

What to Do When Your Software "Dies"

One of the best things about software engineering is that it's so easy for those tech guys to innovate and create more and better functionality. Hooray for progress.

On the other hand, that's also one of the more frustrating characteristics of the software industry. You've got this great software application, you've used it well for years, and then *boom*, one fine day you can't even open it. It won't run on your current operating system, or it's not compatible with your monitor, or something else has gone wrong. Surprise!

It's best to be prepared for these little surprises ahead of time. For example, let's say you were using a 1990s version of your fundraising software. But last summer you replaced all your systems, including an upgrade to the latest version of the Windows operating system. And guess what? The old version of the software won't run on the new version of Windows.

The best way to avoid such glitches is to prepare in advance. If you registered your license to use the software package (and of course you did because otherwise you're breaking the law), you will get an announcement that a new version is coming out. You'll probably also get a promotion to "buy now at a preferred price." Before you hit the delete button, take enough time to figure out if the new version is required, if it will work on your current operating system, and so on. Sometimes you can wait for a later version. For example, QuickBooks comes out with a new version every tax year to accommodate all revisions to the tax code. The older versions will continue to operate for several years, but eventually you will be required to upgrade to the current version. You or the head of your IT department need to be aware that something—a new operating system, new hardware, new CRM product, etc.—will require a major upgrade for one of your current systems. Make sure you budget the money ahead of time.

For hosted systems such as eTapestry, Bloomerang, or Salesforce.com, there are no software upgrades to worry about; the system provider takes care of it. However, you still need to stay up to date about changes in subscription rates, or situations where the provider may un-bundle certain components of the application and then charge you extra for using them.

> Software applications require occasional minor and major upgrades. Sometimes the vendors will even take a product out of circulation (called "sunsetting" the product). Stay ahead of these changes by monitoring your providers' websites and customer communications. If the next revision disables your preferred application or won't run on your hardware or operating system, upgrade before you reach the crisis point.

important

How You Communicate With Funders, Prospects, Volunteers, Clients, Staff, Board, and Others

The engine that drives your communications is, of course, your CRM system. After all, if you don't have anybody to talk to, you don't need to communicate in the first place. But for the most part, the CRM system is only the tool that *distributes* communications; it's not the tool kit that *creates* them.

So the second mission-critical function that technology must play for you is that of communications. Communications includes a very wide range of methods, functions, and technologies. The primary functions you'll want to master are:

- ◆ Your web presence

- ◆ Outbound communications, including emails, email marketing, and blogs

- ◆ Use of social media

Your Website

Your agency must have a presence on the Internet. Period. You may not need an office, a neon sign, or your name on the Goodyear Blimp, but you absolutely, positively have to have a website. The website includes a combination of static or so-called "evergreen" information, but it also should provide ways to provoke responses and interactions from visitors and content that changes fairly frequently.

Like everything else in the world of technology, the technologies that are used to create, update, and interact with websites have been transformed so much, and so rapidly, that virtually anyone with a little patience can create a memorable, functional site. So it's not the technology itself that defines what you can do; it's your mind, creativity, and marketing savvy.

When you set up your website, you need to keep a few things in mind:

- ◆ Who's your audience?

- ◆ How are visitors going to find you in the vast, unbounded universe of the Internet, and what can you do to make it easier for them to do so?

- ◆ Once they find you, is it easy for them to explore your website and move from place to place seeking more information?

- ◆ What information, language, or instructions will provoke a response from your visitors?

- ◆ How will you know they responded, and what will you do then?

If you answer these questions first, you will build a better, more effective, and more attractive website that will produce much better results. For the time being, don't even think about how "pretty" your website should look. That part, surprisingly, is fairly easy.

Benefits of a Content Management System

Once again, innovations in technology give great benefits to nonprofit organizations. One of the most beneficial is the content management system, or CMS. A CMS is a simple way for an ordinary person to update a website even if the individual has no computer skills to speak of. CMS systems typically let you get into the innards of your website and edit pages pretty much as easily as you would make changes to an ordinary Word document. They let you add images, post videos, set up forms that let readers download white papers, and even handle your online donations page without needing to rely on a computer genius (or waiting for that genius to get around to your job). If you've ever noticed a glaring typo on your website, waited three weeks for "the website guy" to fix it, then been astounded when you got the bill, you'll know why a CMS is such a valuable asset.

Changing your website contents frequently is also an excellent way to get noticed more often on the Internet.

Internet Basics

The first thing you need to understand about the Internet is that it is a vast, limitless, invisible universe populated by hundreds of millions of sites, each of which is likely to appeal to some portion of the human population or another. The trick for you is to make your website as visible and popular as possible among your constituents so that you stand out from the crowd.

Think of it this way. Every time a person goes to your website, that's the equivalent of a vote. The more votes you get, the more popular your site becomes, which makes it easier to find the site. And easier and easier. To maintain the relative prominence of your position, you need to constantly do stuff to your site to keep it popular and get more votes over time.

Some extremely simple things you need to do to keep your site more visible and prominent:

◆ Change the copy on your site frequently. The technology used by search engines is aware, through some form of technological magic, when a website shows frequent changes in its copy. Frequent changes raise the popularity ranking of your site.

◆ Use keyword-rich copy. Find out the kinds of terms people are likely to use when they're looking for you. For example, if you run a no-kill animal shelter, you need to put those exact words into your website copy several times on each page. This might violate the way you were trained to write, but it really helps attract the right visitors when you do so.

◆ Set up inbound links. Another thing the search-engine spiders look for is links pointing *toward* your website. Ask your colleagues to include a link to your site in their blogs or newsletters. Refer your social-network contacts back to your website frequently.

◆ Sprinkle the site with methods of interaction. Include "contact us" forms, surveys, ways to download white papers, etc. All of these methods of interaction let you capture contact information from followers and produce more votes that make your site more prominent.

The more visits (votes), interactions, copy changes, and effective use of keywords, the higher your site goes in terms of rankings. The higher the rankings, the larger your following.

Some More Internet Lore

◆ *The role of search engines:* Search engines such as Google are prerequisites for finding stuff on the Internet. Something like 80 percent of all users of the Internet start with a search. These fascinating tools sort through an astonishing amount of information all over the world in milliseconds and give you back pages and pages of references (links) to the sites you're looking for. Your job is to make it easy for search engines to find *your* website.

◆ *Search engine optimization (SEO):* SEO is the combination of methods that raise the ranking of your website in the search engines. To optimize the ranking, you need to update copy frequently, make sure there are lots of links pointing to your website, and use keywords and phrases liberally throughout your website copy. Use common words and phrases that describe your mission, purpose, and area of expertise. Use keyword suggestion tools to find such words and phrases. If you were taught in school to try to use unusual words in your writing, you might have to struggle with this concept a little (we certainly did), but the more common the search term, the more likely people will be to use it.

◆ *Organic versus paid search.* You can buy search terms using technologies such as Google "Ad Words." If you are the highest bidder for such terms, or in the top ten, then when the seeker enters the term, a reference to your site comes up in the form of a little advertisement, usually located in the upper right-hand portion of your monitor. Every time someone uses the search term in question, you get billed for the usage. (You set up a prepaid account, and the search-engine company draws down from your balance.)

For organic searches, you don't have to pay to use the words or phrases; you just sprinkle them heavily in your copy. Organic searches produce lists that appear in the middle of your monitor, just below the search terms.

Each approach has its merits.

The Donor Persona: Who's Visiting Your Website?

An easy way to plan your website is to think of the types of people you want to attract to it, then decide what that category or type is likely looking for. Some Internet marketing experts refer to a type, or category, of visitor as the "buyer" or "donor persona." You need to think of these different personae as you develop website copy and navigation.

Every nonprofit has different constituencies, including the client or user of services, the funding community, staff, board and prospective board members, and so on. Let's use a college as an example. The college's website needs to appeal to aspiring students, so it has to show attractive photographs of campus life, information about curriculum and professors, athletic and social programs, and so on, all the things that would interest a student in attending the school. But the parents of those students may also want some other information, such as the level of security and safety they can anticipate, the availability of religious institutions, financial aid, and support for the student's physical and emotional health.

Then let's think about alumni and prospective donors. What is it they need to see or hear to encourage them to give? And let's not overlook the academics and administrators who may be seeking jobs.

Somehow, the college's website must appeal to, and provide information for, each of these personalities. You must do the same thing with your site.

Email Marketing and Blogs

Your website is the keystone of your communications strategy, but it simply can't do the outbound work of connecting you to your constituencies. For that, you need electronic mail, email marketing, and other technology tools such as blogging.

By the way, email marketing is one of the functions that overlaps with your CRM solution, since its database is the repository of your subscription list.

Although some social-media gurus consider electronic mail to be old school, it remains a reliable, low-cost way to communicate with your donors. If at all possible, see if you can "teach" your CRM database to keep track of the emails you exchange with your contacts. Some systems actually attach copies of all their email messages to the person's contact record, which is an efficient way to keep track of your ongoing conversation with that person.

Email Marketing Systems

Email marketing systems produce electronic newsletters and other forms of mass mailing such as event invitations. Electronic newsletters are invaluable for several reasons:

◆ *Cost:* Electronic newsletters cost almost nothing per outbound email. The major e-newsletter services such as Constant Contact and I-Contact provide 10,000 outbound emails a month for about fifteen dollars, and they offer discounts to nonprofits. Some services like MailChimp are free up to a certain number of records.

◆ *Ease of use*. It's extremely simple to master the use of these services. They often provide predesigned templates that can do the job for most organizations. Entering your unique copy is pretty much like using a word-processing system.

◆ *Calls to action*. An e-newsletter is set up like a regular newsletter, so you can put several different articles in it. Each article should include a call to action, some method that motivates the reader to take actions such as clicking on a link to your website, signing up for the race, registering for the event, making a pledge, etc.

◆ *User-managed subscriptions*. Readers can unsubscribe or change contact information on their own, without asking you to do it for them.

◆ *Impact on search*. If you put some links in the newsletter that point back to your website, all those links will raise your site in search-engine rankings.

To get the most out of email marketing, be consistent. Send out your emails predictably and reliably on a particular schedule, even if it's just once a quarter. You can reuse old articles. I promise you, your readers are not memorizing them.

Blogging

According to Wikipedia, a blog is "a discussion or informational site published on the World Wide Web and consisting of discrete entries ('posts') typically displayed in reverse chronological order (the most recent post appears first)." Blogs are more interactive than newsletters; they invite comments by users that can be displayed along with the original posting. Often you'll get comments on comments! All this interactivity has a positive impact on your following, your popularity, and the search-engine ranking that you'll obtain for your website.

Most blog postings are graphically simple and relatively short, with 200–250 words being a decent size. Writing a blog tends to be an easier, quicker task than putting together a whole newsletter. Depending on your enthusiasm, skills, and interests, you can also create video versions of blogs (called "vlogs," though we can't seem to pronounce that odd word) and podcasts, which are audio recordings that your followers can listen to and download.

Social Networking

The use of social networking emerged first around 2005, and these tools have become ubiquitous in record time. We're sorry if you don't understand or feel comfortable using them, but they are dominating the field of communications technology. If you're not on board with them, you're missing out. Some social-media sites, such as Facebook, are even outpacing conventional email as a communications tool, at least in some circles.

Social networking tools include such familiar animals as Facebook, Twitter, YouTube, and LinkedIn, but there are others coming on-stream all the time. All of these tools can be used at no cost, although several of them (LinkedIn, YouTube, Vimeo, to name a few) offer premium-level subscriptions at a price. But the real cost of social networking is in the time you need to devote to them, not the subscription cost.

The social-media landscape continues to evolve very rapidly. In addition to the new players that come on the scene fairly often, there are many tools and tricks and ways to use these functions, and the faster you can master them, the better off you will be. For the most part, social-media tools are simple to implement, but there is always more to learn. There are also many social-media mavens who offer free and low-cost tips, webinars, and other services. Do a few Google searches to find a couple that you like and follow them regularly.

Meanwhile, take these steps if you haven't done so yet:

- ◆ Set up a Facebook business page for your nonprofit. Do it now. It takes five minutes.

- ◆ Set up a Twitter account. It's free and it takes three minutes.

- ◆ Set up a LinkedIn account. It's free and it takes four minutes.

- ◆ The more you tweet, update LinkedIn, and post messages on your Facebook wall, the faster you'll build a following.

- ◆ Add all of these methods for connecting with you to your standard email signature.

◆ Make sure your website has a "Follow Me" or "Follow Us" form that's easy to find on several or all of your pages. You'll find simple tools for doing so on Facebook, Twitter, and LinkedIn.

◆ Set up your email marketing service and your blog to link to your social-media accounts. That way, every time you publish a new newsletter or blog posting, there'll be a tweet or Facebook notice with a link to the newsletter or blog (and more links back to your website).

◆ Use services such as "HootSuite" to broadcast a message to all your social media sites in one fell swoop.

◆ Don't kill yourself trying to write deathless prose. Speak in your own voice. That's what attracts the following.

How You Manage the Money

The last major business function that must be automated is how you manage the money. For most nonprofits, there are two important categories of financial management—fund accounting and general accounting.

Fund Accounting

This set of functions covers the way you recognize income, draw down grants and appropriations, make use of major and individual donations, utilize corporate sponsorship income, and—last but not least—report on how you did so. You'll also use this functional area to keep track of and handle sales of fee-for-service contracts and product sales if you offer them.

Fund accounting is analogous to the way sales companies handle sales income but naturally includes a variety of other specialized functions relevant to the nonprofit sector. A key example is that of the reporting requirements that are frequently imposed by grantors, who may require a detailed accounting of the ways in which every dollar and percentage of the whole was allocated and any exceptions justified or accounted for.

There is a natural relationship or overlap between the CRM system and the fund-accounting functions, especially in terms of the major blocks of income from major or planned gifts, grants, and appropriations. Not only does each such gift have implications for accounting but also for acknowledgment, recognition, and other reporting to the funder.

General Accounting

Nonprofits must also keep track of the money spent on the operating budget, payroll, employee benefits, liability insurance, and any relevant taxation. Many mainstream accounting packages include versions that have been specialized to meet the general and fund-accounting needs of nonprofit organizations.

TMI! Or How Do We Figure Out What We Need?

Information technology can be either a black hole attracting tons of dollars and giving nothing back or a boon to mankind as valuable as indoor plumbing. Here are some simple guidelines to help you navigate your way to a good outcome.

◆ Think "What do I need to accomplish?" rather than "Do I want this cool new thing I heard about on the news last night?" Rely on your strategic plan and other well-articulated goals and objectives. Do your research based on this information, and manage your vendors in a similar way.

◆ Spend the time it takes to define your requirements. Don't let your vendors do that for you (although you should encourage their input).

◆ Think "What will it cost me *not* to have this technology?" instead of "It costs too much."

◆ Use your CRM system and communications technologies to find, cultivate, attract, and get to know likely prospects. Don't let them get lost in the shuffle.

◆ Highly effective technology can actually keep down your payroll costs, will definitely reduce your postage costs, and will likely increase your income from gifts and grants, if you let it.

◆ Think "cost of ownership" rather than "finding a cheap product." Sometimes a more expensive ticket price gives you better support, better service, and more functionality than a cheaper price tag might be able to do. If it's low cost to get into the product but then you end up paying lots of money to stay current, fix what's broken, or get somebody to show you how to use it, what's happening to your budget?

Be open-minded as you review your options. Just because the product is well known and/or has a lot of "bells and whistles" doesn't mean it will meet your needs. You might need to have separate systems to handle separate functions; you might be able to find one software provider whose applications support all your needs.

The better you understand your business information needs and preferences, the more likely you will be to find a vendor or service provider who is sympathetic, understands your needs, shares your corporate values, and has a vested interest in *your* success, not just a commission check.

To Recap

◆ Every function in your nonprofit business will be supported by technology of one sort or another. Fundraising may be the single most technology-intensive business function of them all, so understanding the ramifications of your fundraising needs is paramount.

◆ Spend the time it takes to make sense out of your needs. Work with mentors, consultants, and other advisors if you need their help in defining your requirements.

◆ Don't "cheap out" when it comes to technology. Spending the right amount of money on the right technological solution will be more likely to get you the fundraising returns you want and need. Doing otherwise, even if the ticket price is low, will probably end up costing you a king's ransom, setting you back years, and even "ticking off" your donors when you don't get their information correct.

Chapter Four

Performance Metrics, Benchmarks, and Guidelines

IN THIS CHAPTER

---→ Why good performance metrics are important

---→ What you can measure, what you can't, and what you should

---→ Indicators, success measures, and performance targets: why you need all three

---→ How performance metrics convert the subjective into the objective and why that's helpful

Everybody likes to talk about performance metrics, but the why and how of measuring performance? That's not always so clear. This chapter will give you a useful overview of the concepts and vocabulary of measuring performance so you can manage it.

Good measurements, or metrics, enable you to manage your own work effectively, get the best results from your team, and make it easier to produce predictable, consistent results from complex business functions such as development.

The Leaky Bucket study assessed several issues relating to metrics for fundraising, including total income, income by category, visits with donors, and number of grant applications or proposals produced. These are the most basic of the basic metrics. Yet the most frequently used metric, total income, was used by only 63 percent of respondents, and only 14 percent said they kept track of number of visits with donors. Development is an area that cries out for more effective measurement—and it provides many useful things that could be measured easily.

The manufacturing industry started to use performance metrics back in the mid-twentieth century, and ever since then, manufacturers have gotten better and better at improving productivity, reducing cost, shortening the time it takes to produce goods, and so on. But development shops are not assembly lines, and lots of things happen in the development effort that don't seem particularly easy to measure. Or maybe they're not objective enough to measure. But we're happy to tell you that when it comes to fundraising, there are plenty of things that you can measure. And you don't have to measure them with a microscope either.

Managing Performance—Why Measuring Stuff Is Important

If you can't measure it, you can't manage it. And if you can't manage it, you can't improve its productivity. Since nonprofit professionals are always trying to do more with less, it pays to figure out what to measure so you can increase efficiency and effectiveness. Greater efficiency and effectiveness translate into greater productivity, meaning you can accomplish more and better results with the same (or fewer) resources. And don't all our boards and CEOs expect that?

> Inexact measurements of the *right* things are more meaningful than exact measurements of the wrong things.

important

Many nonprofit organizations do a good job of measuring the performance of their programs. Outcome measurements are common in many nonprofit sectors and are often required by the funder. Unfortunately, fundraising is rarely included in discussions about performance improvement.

What You Can Measure

If you can count it, meet a deadline, or calculate a percentage, you can measure it. Some things are easy to measure but not very important (such as how many phone calls you make), while others are more difficult to measure, but tell you a lot of important stuff (such as how many donor prospects are interested in your cause or mission). The ideal situation is to have a reasonable number of measurements that are highly "diagnostic," which means that they tell you important things about performance.

There are only five ways to measure performance. If you can't measure your chosen indicators with one of these methods, then you need to redefine the indicator or choose another one. The methods are:

> Of all nonprofits surveyed, only 63 percent measure total income and 47 percent measure income by category (grants, major gifts, corporate relations, etc.) Fourteen percent keep track of visits with donors, and 24 percent keep track of number of grant applications or proposals produced. And 13 percent chose "none of the above."
>
> **leaky bucket results**

♦ *Numbers of items, occurrences, or observations:* Examples: number of times a donor-prospect agrees to accept your proposal for a major gift; number of times major donors refer you to other prospects.

♦ *Amount, percentages, ratios.* Examples: amount of income in a given month, percentage of total income received from grants, ratio between donor prospects who have agreed to an initial meeting and those who have pledged a certain amount (also called a conversion ratio).

♦ *Yes/no/always/never:* Examples: phone calls from donor prospects are *always* referred to the development office; development officers *always* update the donor-management software; board members *never* go out on prospecting calls without a development officer.

♦ *Deadline:* Examples: the venue for next year's gala must be contracted *by June 1*; requests for travel reimbursements must be filed *no later than the 20th of every month.*

♦ *Turnaround times:* Examples: gifts of any size must be acknowledged *within twenty-four hours of receipt.*

What You *Can't* Measure

It's impossible to measure abstractions such as team spirit or all-encompassing ideas like success. Instead of trying to measure these elusive ideas, ask yourself "What would I have to see or hear to know that we were working as a team?" or "What would I have to see or hear to know that we are successful?" Indirect evidence often provides rich indicators.

Now we are not saying that you don't want to achieve a high level of team spirit; of course you do. But you can't measure it. What you *can* measure, instead, is some observable evidence that people are working together effectively, or whatever abstract concept you seek. The observable evidence can serve as a performance indicator, as long as the indicator can be

---

A large community development corporation had two staff members who handled mortgage lending, one to obtain loan applications from clients, and the other to process them. The loan processor complained that the loan originator submitted incomplete paperwork. The loan originator complained that the processor didn't file the information on time. Clients were unhappy. The board chair demanded, "For heaven's sake, what's wrong with you guys? You're supposed to be team players!!! Fix it!!!!"

The executive director realized that yelling at her staff wouldn't do much. So she solved the problem by assigning two measurements that were tracked at the same time. One said "All loan applications submitted for processing must be submitted in complete form," and the other, "All applications will be processed within three business days after submission." The target for ideal performance was "100 percent compliance," and both employees were accountable for reaching the target. The executive director then said that she would review their joint performance once a week.

Within eight weeks, the two-person team was performing beyond expectations. Client satisfaction improved, internal tension disappeared, and the board chair was delighted.

 **stories from the real world**

---

measured by one of the five types of measurement above. If you can't boil it down to one of those measuring methods, you can't track it. And if you can't track (or measure) it, you can't manage or improve it, right?

What You *Should* Measure

When managing performance, you need to strike a balance between too few measurements and too many. As we said before, you could conceivably measure dozens or hundreds of different things, but to what end? That's why we prefer to measure *results* wherever possible, not just activities.

Results are the observable outcomes of activity. There are always fewer results to measure than there are activities, especially in the development organization. It's easier to track (and make sense of) six or seven results than twenty or thirty activities.

When you measure results, you empower your people to choose the tactics and activities that seem right for them and for each situation, as long as the tactics chosen are ethical and cost effective. An empowered workforce tends to be happier and more productive. By assigning metrics based on results, it's as if you're saying, "As long as you achieve the results desired and don't violate our ethics, values, or budgets, you can do anything you want to get the job done." Staff members thrive on such leadership.

Good Examples of Results

Good examples of results include:

◆ *Total number of opportunities currently active in the pipeline:* This is a result because you already did the work to identify the opportunity and begin the work of cultivation.

◆ *Total number of new donors acquired per month:* This is a result because your development team has already done the work of cultivation.

◆ *Proportion of funding per funding category:* Keeping track of the level of fund diversification is clearly a result and not an activity.

◆ *Growth in size of your newsletter subscription list.* Ditto.

Anatomy of a Performance Indicator

Performance indicators, also called key performance indicators or KPIs, have three components: the item being measured, the method of measuring, and the performance target. They also have an additional attribute: information about the indicator must be relatively easy to capture. Let's use driving on the interstate as an example of a classic performance indicator.

Good performance indicators meet these criteria:

◆ *They are diagnostic.* They tell you something you need to know, preferably something that reveals the effectiveness or efficiency of the process.

◆ *They are easy to capture.* You can document or keep track of them without a lot of hassle.

◆ *They guide or have an impact on behavior.* When your team does or does not behave according to these indicators, performance will be affected one way or another.

> Signs along the interstate post the local speed limit. They describe what to measure, namely the speed at which you are driving. They state the method of measurement, miles (or kilometers) per hour. They set the performance target (55 mph, 100 kph, etc.). Whether you choose to obey the speed limit is up to you.
>
> **Example**

◆ *Some of your chosen indicators are "leading," and some are "trailing" or "lagging."* You have a method for observing performance details at several points along the continuum of the process as well as what happens at the tail end of the process. That way, you can spot things upstream and fix them before they become unmanageable.

◆ *The performance indicators themselves are quantifiable.* You can count them or keep track of them according to one of the five methods for measurement described above.

Performance Indicators, Benchmarks, Guidelines: What's the Difference?

Performance indicators are the most specific, quantifiable forms of measurement, as we have been describing up to now. They describe the thing being measured, they refer to the method of measurement, and they include a performance target.

There are two other elements that contribute to performance management: benchmarks and guidelines.

Benchmarks

Benchmarks are lists of criteria or characteristics that describe something desirable and can be used as a basis of comparison, like a yardstick. An ideal-funder profile is a good example of a benchmark.

Guidelines

Guidelines are policies, or policy-like statements, that describe preferred methods or mechanisms of getting things done or making critical decisions. Having guidelines in place provides a set of precedents or instructions and avoids reinventing the wheel. Guidelines are pretty much like the "house rules."

To our surprise, the Leaky Bucket study shows that only 63 percent of the nonprofits surveyed set targets for total income, and only 47 percent set targets for income by funding category, a shocking outcome. Even though income is a trailing indicator, it is truly of mission-critical importance. If your nonprofit is not tracking income, ask yourself why. If you think it's demotivating or scary to establish a performance target for total income, you are making a mistake. It's more demotivating not to have such a target, especially when you can see how well you are doing against it.

leaky bucket results

Guideline for Reviewing the Opportunity Pipeline

This is a sample guideline. Note that it refers to a specific set of people ("we"), contains action words ("will review"), and has a timeline ("weekly"). Sounds kind of like a SMART objective, doesn't it?

"We will review the opportunity pipeline weekly to identify areas where the fundraising process encounters obstacles or bottlenecks. Once identified,

Benchmark describing the ideal major donor for XYZ Agency:

◆ Has a net worth of at least $10 million

◆ Has a history of giving at least $25,000 per year to us or similar charities for the past ten years

◆ Has a stated desire to support charities such as ours

Example

we will try to figure out how to remove or reduce the obstacle. We will not spend any time on blame or recriminations and, instead, will focus on where to go from here."

Results Are Just Results; They Are Neither Good Nor Bad

People sometimes feel anxious when they start measuring performance. They worry that they can't meet the targets, so the metrics themselves may feel punitive. But they are not. Performance metrics are something like navigational aids. If you were sailing a boat, you'd want to know if you were on course or off, so you'd look at your compass and navigational charts frequently. If you get off course for any reason, your navigational aids help you get back on course. And you don't yell at your compass.

Think about performance metrics the same way. They help you and your development team stay on course, get back on course if need be, and even discover new and innovative ways to reach their targets. Performance indicators, benchmarks, and guidelines tend to make the "invisible" visible and make the "subjective" more objective. They improve both clarity and accountability.

So, what do you want your various metrics to tell you, anyway? Let them speak. They will tell you one of three things:

◆ The individual or group is meeting its performance targets. If you are happy with that level of performance, then you make efforts to lock in what's working so you can replicate it.

◆ The individual or group is exceeding its performance targets. If that level of performance is desirable, then you make efforts to figure out why it improved and then lock in those methods so you can maintain it.

◆ The individual or group is falling below its performance targets. If you are not happy with that level of performance, then you make efforts to figure out what is not working and repair it. Typically you would attempt to make changes upstream in the process so the results downstream will improve.

To Recap

◆ You can't manage it if you can't measure it, and you can't improve it if you can't measure it.

◆ Knowing what, why, and how to measure the right things in the development function makes a very complicated function less complicated. It takes a lot of guesswork out of the system. It improves motivation and staff engagement or loyalty because now the staff really understands what's expected of them.

◆ Effective, rational, and understandable metrics will empower your development team to perform better and more productively.

Chapter Five

Creating Awareness: Your Case for Support

IN THIS CHAPTER

- ···➔ What makes your nonprofit a good charitable investment?

- ···➔ Guidelines for creating your case statement

- ···➔ A checklist for effective case statements

- ···➔ A checklist for fundraising materials

Your agency's case for support might be complete, succinct, motivating, and up to date. But the Leaky Bucket study has shown that only 22 percent of agencies seem to have one at all and that only 17 percent think of upgrading it if fundraising results fall below desired levels.

The case for support is the basis for all fundraising messages, documents, collateral, flyers, and campaign materials. If you haven't done your homework, created the case for support, and documented it, then you have to reinvent the wheel every time.

Understanding what motivates people to give is a primary concern for fundraising staff. This chapter will help you review your case for support, if you have one, or develop a case if you do not already have one. We will also talk about what materials you should have or create from your case for support.

Developing Your Case for Support: Telling Your Story

One of the first steps in fundraising is to develop a case for support for your organization. All organizations need a well-written case for support. If you don't have one, or it's out of date, now is the perfect opportunity to develop it. The case for support forms the basis of all your fundraising communications, whether printed, verbal, or electronic, and it spawns a variety of case statements that you will use for different purposes. Having a compelling case is the first essential ingredient in effectively communicating your organization's needs to your constituents.

One of the hardest things for many organizations to understand is that people do not support your organization because *you* need the money. Let's face it, *every* nonprofit needs money. What makes your case compelling is answering these simple questions.

◆ How is our organization saving or changing lives?

◆ How is our community or world a better place because our organization exists?

> People don't give to your organization because you *have* needs; they give because your organization is *filling* needs in the community.

important

◆ What would our community be like if our organization ceased to exist?

◆ What is our vision for the future of our community?

◆ How can the donor become involved in being part of the solution?

◆ WIIFM? What's in it for me (the donor)? Why should I support this organization?

Sounds easy, huh?

Well, let's stop a minute. Have your really thought about the answers to these questions? How persuasively have you answered them in your fundraising materials, website, and presentations to potential donors?

Here are some guidelines to get you started.

- ❑ What is our mission?

- ❑ What are our values?

- ❑ What is our vision?

- ❑ Is our mission concise (usually one or two sentences), and does it tell the public what we actually do?

- ❑ Are our values clear, and will they resonate with our potential donors?

- ❑ Is our vision truly visionary and focused on the community rather than internally?

Answer these questions before you begin to write or update your case for support.

What Goes into Your Case?

A preliminary case for support needs to be developed before you start writing any materials that will be used in fundraising, including your website, fundraising letters, and donor solicitation scripts.

Readers of your case will want to know the mission and vision of your organization. What does your organization do, where is it headed, and what are its values? Why is your organization important to the community?

The history of your organization is important, especially when you can show a track record of success. Most donors will not want to support your nonprofit unless they know it can deliver what it promises. If your organization can demonstrate that it has provided successful programs with good outcomes, donors will be motivated to be a part of your future success.

The overall organizational case for support should outline all your programs and services in detail. Individual case statements will then be developed for various appeals. For example, if your university is raising money for a new performing arts center, you will want to focus on the need for expanded programs in this area, the potential audiences for

Some of the key ingredients that will be in your case for support include:

◆ Mission

◆ Vision

◆ History

◆ Current programs and services

◆ List of board and staff members

◆ Financial information

◆ Need for future growth

◆ Plan for addressing these needs

◆ Opportunities for the donor to participate in the vision

 practical tip

these programs, and the benefit to the students and community of this new center. Or, if you are developing a case statement for your annual fund that will support all of your programs, you will want to give a highlight of each program. Or you might be developing a case for planned giving in which you will want to show the reader the benefits of long-term sustainability of your programs through a healthy endowment.

Additional items to be included in the case are lists of board and staff. Make sure to list executive staff and members of the board by name. Prospective donors will be reassured that the organization is in good hands. Show that the staff has the credentials and experience to run the programs. Present a sound financial picture; donors will not want to support a sinking ship. In a case statement for a capital campaign, realistic financial projections that are well thought out will be very persuasive.

For whatever case you are making, there must be a clear need for this project, not related to your organization alone but to the community of which the donor is part. And there must be a logical plan for addressing the needs of your community.

Regardless of the particular campaign or project, your case needs to show that the community will benefit, not just your organization alone. To further reinforce the proposed benefit, your case must propose a logical plan that addresses the issue directly and "makes the case" for investing in your agency.

❑ Does it provide both emotional and rational reasons for the donor to give?

❑ Does it tell your potential donors how their gift will make a difference?

❑ Does it evoke a sense of the history and long-term importance of your organization and its work?

❑ Does it offer proof that your plan will work?

❑ Are the benefits to the donor clearly stated?

❑ If you include graphs or charts, are they striking, accurate, and meaningful?

❑ Is it concise?

❑ Is it oriented to the reader or prospect rather than to your organization?

❑ Does it emphasize opportunity for the donor rather than need of the organization?

❑ Is the information presented in a logical order?

❑ Is it readable with short sentences and paragraphs?

Once your case is ready to be presented in written materials, some additional things to look for are:

❑ Is the typeface appropriate to your organization's appeal?

❑ Is there enough white space to make it easy to read?

❑ Is the type large enough to be read by older prospects?

❑ Is the cover striking?

❑ Is the paper stock attractive without looking expensive?

❑ If you use photographs, are they effective and cropped to maximize their impact? Photos should not include more than two or three people. Large group shots lose dramatic impact. Do you have the proper permissions to use these photos?

Developing Materials from Your Case

Many organizations spend a lot of money on fundraising materials but have not first asked themselves how they will use these materials. It is important to finalize the case before materials are produced and to make sure that they present a uniform look and feel. It is also important not to overemphasize the importance of your written materials. Spending a lot of money on printed materials but not investing time and effort into qualifying your prospective donors will result in a "hole in your bucket."

In a world of Twitter, Facebook, web-based fundraising, and all the other social media and Internet possibilities, you might even ask, "Is there still a place for printed marketing materials to support our development program?"

As with everything else this book discusses about fundraising, we think it all comes down to the key word, *diversify*!

Diversifying your funding streams is critical to a successful development program. Likewise, you should consider diversifying the approaches to your donors. Here are a few potential donor constituencies and some ways they may be best approached, using your case as the basis for these communications.

Foundations

Some foundations want to receive proposals online only, which helps you avoid that last-minute rush to the post office, not to mention producing seventeen bound copies at the all-night copying store. However, deadlines on the Internet cannot be fudged, so be sure you have the proposal written and edited before emailing it to the prospective funder. If the application must be entered into an online proposal system, create, spell-check, and edit it in word-processing mode so you can cut and paste it section by section into the foundation's system.

How else can you communicate with foundations? Foundation program officers will most likely visit your website for any additional information they need, so make sure it is up to date and professionally done. You might also send materials like your annual report to the foundation by mail or provide a link to your annual report and marketing materials on your website, which is the more environmentally conscious (and cheaper) approach.

Corporations and Commercial Businesses

Be clear about the way you approach a corporation or other business. If you are cultivating a gift from a business that does not have a foundation, the owner or decision maker will be more likely to respond to a direct approach. The decision maker might not have the time or interest to search your website or read through tons of written materials. Get right to the point! Use a fact sheet that clearly outlines your organization's programs and the impact you have on the community. Also be sure to include any facts about the way the business will be recognized for its support and what impact its dollars will have on the community. For local businesses, this is a key facet of the approach. A corporation might also want to see your annual report to make sure the bottom line shows that you are an efficient, well-run organization.

If the corporation supports a charitable foundation, your strategy will be similar to that of a private foundation, as discussed above. This foundation will be "in the business" of giving money to nonprofits, and they know how to look for you or respond to you.

Volunteers

When volunteers are invited to contribute financially, it is important to recognize their volunteer contributions. A direct-mail or mail/phone approach can be effective if it is personalized to

---

Materials to be developed from your case include:

❑ Brochures

❑ Leadership case statements

❑ Foundation proposals

❑ Website

❑ Email and direct-mail letters

❑ Phone scripts

❑ Scripts to use on in-person calls

❑ Speeches

❑ Volunteer training materials

❑ Fact sheets

❑ Videos/DVDs

❑ PowerPoint presentation

❑ Annual report

❑ Support materials such as pledge cards, response envelopes, and stationery

practical tip

the volunteer, signed by a volunteer, and stresses the importance of both the volunteer's time and monetary gifts. Volunteers might not need fancy brochures because they are already familiar with your organization, but you might want to direct them to your website to see all the work your organization is doing beyond the programs with which they may already be familiar. If you do this, be sure that your website thanks and recognizes the volunteers who are involved.

Clients/Users of Your Services/Alumni/Parents, Etc.

This group, as with your volunteers, will already be familiar with your organization and will likely respond to a personalized approach such as those mentioned above. Solicitations sent by email, with links that allow them to give online, can be especially effective. Of course, the website must have an online donation page that is easy to find, is easy to use, and gives the prospect a variety of gift options and levels.

Major-Gift Prospects

Although major donors generally come from the donor pool of people who already support your organization, they should be treated as a special group. Their gifts are usually considerably larger than the average individual or online gift. The process of soliciting these larger gifts must be personalized and individualized. These individuals usually like to be on the "inside track" and acknowledged for their greater level of commitment and involvement. It can be helpful to prepare personalized case statements for these individuals as part of your cultivation efforts. Make sure that the cultivation strategy shows your desire to gain their input on the project in question, not just their dollars.

The General Public

It is fairly common to discover that nonprofits invest in the most expensive marketing materials and direct-mail campaigns as a strategy to approach the general public. But we ask, "Does this strategy produce the greatest number of gifts and the highest amount of income?" If not, is it worth spending tons of money on glitzy brochures, videos, etc.? Consider several factors when you're deciding what kinds of campaigns to use to attract donations from the public at large:

◆ Your budget, of course. Do you have the money to invest in this donor pool using these means? Are there other means that are more compatible with your budget?

◆ The level of market awareness your organization enjoys in the community. If no one knows who you are, you might be better off investing money to improve that awareness.

◆ The amount of money you need to raise. When your organization runs a capital campaign, the dollar target is usually considerable, often in the millions. In such a case, the dollar amount of the goal may easily justify the cost of expensive collateral materials.

◆ The nature of your organization. A museum, hospital, or university can usually get away with more upscale fundraising materials, but a human services agency might turn people off if its materials appear to be too elaborate or expensive.

So how do you decide what the key elements of your collateral materials should be? Here are some steps that can help.

◆ Have a compelling, well-branded case for support. All your materials should come from this case statement and share a uniform look, sound, and feel.

◆ Determine who your audiences are and what motivates them to give to charities such as yours. There might be more stakeholders than you think!

◆ Determine what types of materials are best for each constituency, how many of each of these materials you will need, and how much they will cost.

◆ Determine your budget and decide how much is appropriate to invest in each constituency.

◆ Look for ways to produce your materials economically. Ask printers or designers to make in-kind donations of their services. Find a donor to underwrite the cost of a video.

Collateral Materials

What should be the key elements of your collateral materials program? We suggest:

◆ The case for support

◆ A top-notch website

◆ An annual report

◆ Leadership case statements for major donors

◆ PowerPoint presentation for group presentations

◆ Brochures

◆ Stationery and envelopes

◆ Fact sheets

◆ Video, CD, or DVD

◆ Pledge cards, response envelopes, letters of intent

In some cases, additional collateral material may be helpful, such as bookmarks, recognition pieces, giveaways, etc. But always start with the two key ingredients: *a powerful case statement and a dynamite website!*

To Recap

◆ Before designing a website, printing brochures, or writing grant proposals, you need to have a compelling case for support. From this case will be developed various case statements to support the fundraising for various aspects of your development program and all the materials that you will need to make your case to your constituents.

◆ Using the checklist, make sure your case is rational *and* emotional, and be sure it is donor centered.

◆ Your case should always be tested with your constituents to make sure it is compelling.

◆ Develop appropriate materials for each of your constituent audiences.

Chapter Six

Creating Awareness: PR and Branding

IN THIS CHAPTER

- ┅➔ Strategic marketing: what you offer and to whom

- ┅➔ The wide range of methods for getting the word out about your nonprofit

- ┅➔ Establishing your brand

- ┅➔ The buyer persona: who's looking at your stuff?

- ┅➔ Using social media

Ellen's informal Leaky Bucket study does not measure any specifics about nonprofit public relations, branding, and cultivation, except for one critical issue: whether you have an up-to-date case statement. Only 17 percent of study participants said that they had a case statement that was up to date. (See **Chapter Five** on "Your Case for Support.")

That's pretty dismal. The case statement embodies your marketing proposition, sometimes called the unique value proposition (UVP), and its key messages. A good, well-written case statement is the basis of all your marketing, because it tells your story so well. And the purpose of marketing is to tell your story!

If you haven't documented your case for support, or if it's out of date, your marketing strategy is already limping. It's easy to go wrong with your marketing, PR, and branding. Here are some other examples we've noticed that reveal ineffective branding:

◆ Websites created without the use of keywords and search terms, which means fewer visitors to the site

◆ Websites that use color schemes and images that don't appear on stationery or collateral

◆ Online donation pages that lack calls to action, suggested giving levels, or descriptions of how gifts will be used

◆ Poor website navigation

◆ Websites that don't contain enough ways to interact, such as "contact us" forms, newsletter subscriptions, ability to download white papers, and so on

◆ Mission descriptions that are unclear, or that are phrased differently on different website pages, brochures, annual report, etc.

◆ Inconsistent use of newsletters, blog postings, or other outbound marketing activities

◆ Websites that are not kept up to date and still have the dates and locations of last year's gala or old board of directors lists

◆ Websites that do not contain basic information such as address, phone number, board members, key staff, and a method to contact the organization's staff

◆ Unclear marketing strategy; unclear social-media strategy; unclear branding strategy

◆ Failure to review website usage reports and use them to improve site performance

Marketing: The New Rules

Before the advent of Facebook, Twitter, and the global reach of the Internet, there were only a few ways to get the word out about your nonprofit, and most of them were costly. You might use traditional public relations to get mentioned in the media: print/radio/TV advertising, and direct mail.

Today the array of potential marketing mechanisms is enormous, the cost of entry for most of them is pretty low, and if you don't use at least some of them, you're taking a risk. This chapter is designed to give you some guidelines for the strategic side of your marketing efforts along with a brief review of the various mechanisms at your disposal.

> Keep your case statement up to date and easy to find. You should use it to create website copy, newsletter articles, blog postings, your annual report, and many other marketing tactics.
>
>
> **important**

Marketing 101: Understanding the Basics

Understand a few basics of marketing before you start putting campaigns together. Get this basic stuff right first, and then it's easier to create the flyers, brochures, website copy, and direct-mail pieces you'll need.

Who's Your Audience? The Donor Persona

First and perhaps most important: Who are you talking to anyway? Different audiences respond to different types of messages. Plus you'll want these different audiences to respond to you in different ways. You'll want prospective donors to give you gifts, clients to enroll in your programs, and others (staff, board, volunteers?) to join your team.

Marketers in the for-profit world use a concept called the buyer persona, a term that describes the different types of buyers they wish to appeal to in their websites and other marketing tactics. We call it donor persona for our nonprofit sector. Please review **Chapter Three** for more details on this concept.

You always have at least three distinctive personae or personalities that you want to speak to and sometimes more. One is the potential funder, of course. You'll want to develop messages that persuade different types of funders to take an interest in your organization.

Second is your potential client. You need to have messages that attract the people or families or other populations that you serve with your programs.

The third category is made up of prospective employees, volunteers, or board members. Depending on the size and maturity of your organization, you might end up needing more than three categories here.

Sit down and think about what each of these personae wants to hear from you. What will inspire them to pick up the phone and get hold of you, write a check, apply for a job, or volunteer their time?

Think about the types of visitor you want to attract to your organization through your website and other marketing mechanisms. List each type of visitor and define a few characteristics for each. Ask yourself which information or message would appeal to each type of website visitor.

◆ *The client or prospective client*: What types of individuals or families or client-like populations do you serve? What do they want to know about you, and what do you want to know about them?

◆ *The individual donor*: What's characteristic of your typical individual donors? What do they want, need, and expect to learn about you—and what do you want to know about them?

◆ *The major donor*: If your nonprofit is ready to work with major donors and gifts, what's characteristic of major donors? What do they want to know that's different from your other donors? What will persuade them to take action?

◆ *Grantmaking organizations*: Don't get lazy about grants-based funding and expect that you need only to read the foundation's published granting guidelines. Find out what your best grantmakers want to know about your organization as well as what you'd like to know about them.

◆ *Corporate philanthropy*: Are you ready to seek gifts or grants from corporate foundations? If so, ask yourself similar questions that you'd ask to attract private foundations.

◆ *Corporate sponsorships*: Corporate sponsorships differ from corporate philanthropy in several ways. The biggest difference is that the corporate sponsorship is viewed by the company as an integral portion of its own marketing strategies, and it may not be tax deductible as a charitable contribution. Make sure your website strategy offers some motivating information to prospective corporate sponsors. See **Chapter Fourteen** for more details on this.

The Call to Action

Now that you've figured out whom you're addressing with your marketing messages, think about the call to action. If your marketing materials can't persuade your target-market audience to take action, it doesn't matter how much time or money you've spent on them.

The call to action persuades the visitor or reader to *do* something. Do you want the reader to reply to you? Give you a donation? Read your white paper? Enroll in your program? It's up to you to spell out the actions you want these readers or visitors to take.

One of the many benefits of electronic marketing techniques is that they can offer so many different calls to action. You can vary the language frequently, set up alternate approaches to test their performance, and change them whenever you want.

Some classic actions that you'll want your visitors/readers to take include the following:

◆ *Sign up for your newsletters or blogs.* This helps you build your valuable database of followers, people who may later become donors or clients or even board members.

◆ *Download a white paper or report.* This also captures contact information. Plus it tells you something about the visitor's interests.

◆ *"Contact us" forms.* These forms encourage visitors to ask a question or request a call back. This call to action indicates that the visitor has a real interest in connecting with your nonprofit. (Be careful to scrutinize the visitor's contact information. You'll probably get lots of people who want to sell you lists or other services; you're not required to respond if you don't want to.)

In interactive or electronic marketing, these calls to action are often referred to as conversions. That means that the visitor views the particular website page or blog or whatever it is and converts to another action.

Keywords and Search Terms: Why Common Language Works Better

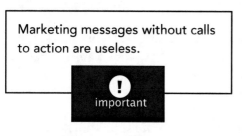

Marketing messages without calls to action are useless.

Keywords and search terms are critical to telling your story.

A search term is a word or phrase that is used to look something up on the Internet. You enter the term in a search engine like Google, and you get back a list of references or links to relevant sites or articles. Use familiar words or phrases as your search terms and keywords because those are the ones used most often by the searchers.

Place these keywords and search terms into the body of your marketing copy, white papers, or e-newsletters, and make sure they are part of the title. When writing blogs or updating your website contents, you may also be able to set up a list of keywords, metatags, and descriptions, as well as use the terms in the copy.

Learn how to use keyword suggestion tools. These electronic tools can help you figure out which terms are used more often. We have listed a number of keyword suggestion tools in **Appendix A**, and you can find them yourself by Googling the phrase "keyword suggestion tools."

Build Your Community

As we've said earlier, these days you have dozens of ways to tell your story and get the word out. But you also need to understand that people encounter literally tens of thousands of marketing messages every day (hour?). So somehow you've got to attract the individuals who *want* to know about you, your nonprofit, and the cause you represent. Now you can start to get creative. Here are a few major outlets for building a following.

Electronic Newsletters

E-newsletters are fairly easy to create and highly cost effective. They are extremely impactful because their costs are low (no postage) and they are (relatively) easy to use. The major electronic newsletter services give you analytical reports about who's reading, clicking on, and forwarding your publications.

Make sure you create interesting copy with lots of search terms. You can tell your story over and over, you can make meaningful announcements, you can—and should—include heartwarming success stories, and so on. E-newsletters allow you to create several separate stories, just like a conventional printed newsletter.

Make sure that your newsletter includes the following components:

We went to a free site called www.keyworddiscovery.com and entered the search term "fundraising." We immediately got a list of the top one hundred search terms. The most frequently used terms were "fundraising/ fundraiser," at 544 hits in the last month. The least frequently used term was "4H fundraising ideas," at five hits in the last month.

That means 544 people would find your website if you used the terms "fundraising" and "fundraiser" and only five people would find you if you used "4H fundraising ideas." However, if you want to appeal specifically to 4H groups, it might be wise to use both of these keywords.

Example

◆ Attractive and easy-to-read appearance that's consistent with your website's graphic look and feel, corporate colors, and images

◆ Your logo and mission statement

◆ Options provided by the newsletter service, including "join our mailing list," "forward to a friend," "manage your subscription" (where readers can update their own email address and preferences and can unsubscribe)

◆ Calls to action with links back to your website, such as "Sign up for our next event," "Read this white paper," and so on

Most newsletter services also offer the option of archiving your newsletter so you can revive an edition and circulate it again so readers can always look up the back copies.

Blogs

A blog is a great way to interact with your readers and have a dialog with them, something the conventional e-newsletter doesn't do nearly as well. Most blogging services are free; the most popular ones at this time are Wordpress and Blogspot. Blogs allow the reader to post comments, so now your followers can engage in a conversation with you and with one another. Most blog postings address a single topic.

To make your blog attractive, include the following:

◆ Keyword-rich title and copy

◆ Use of metatags and metadescriptions, another way to utilize keywords and search terms

◆ An image or two. Blogs containing images are more likely to be read than those without.

◆ Adequate length. Blog postings longer than 250 words engage more readers than shorter ones.

◆ Links back to your website, including calls to action

◆ Consistent use. Send out a new blog posting at least once a week. It takes a while to build a following, and the more frequently you post a new blog, the faster you'll build it.

Social Media

Social media tools have transformed the marketing landscape profoundly, and they are only going to become more sophisticated and more omnipresent than they are today. So if your nonprofit does not have a Facebook business page, a Twitter account, a YouTube account, or a presence in many of the other sites and services, you are cutting yourself off from a huge population. If anyone needs further persuading, remember that the 2011 uprising in Egypt, which resulted in the rapid overthrow of a long-standing, dictatorial regime, was fomented largely through the use of Facebook. Facebook and the other social media tools are incredibly powerful at creating a sense of community and fostering immediate two-way communication between the brand and the brand's following.

It's not in the scope of this manual to teach you how to utilize social media, but it is in your best interests to understand the basics. Social media make it easy for you to:

◆ tell your story in your own voice;

◆ create a following;

◆ communicate directly with your constituents;

◆ get immediate feedback from your constituents; and

◆ involve your constituents in marketing for you.

Start your social-media strategy by establishing a Facebook page, a Twitter account, and a LinkedIn profile. These tools are currently the most influential in the nonprofit sector. All three services are free. Free of cost, that is; you'll still need to invest enough time in them to make them work for you. If you expect to have a lot of videos, set up a YouTube or Vimeo account as well.

Branding

We Googled the question "What is branding?" and found this great definition from the American Marketing Association. It says that "a brand [is] a name, term, sign, symbol, or design, or a combination of them intended to identify the goods and services of one seller or group of sellers and to differentiate them from those of other sellers." If we just replace the term "sellers" with the term "nonprofits," this definition works perfectly well for fundraising purposes.

Branding allows your constituents to understand why your nonprofit is a good choice for them, whether they are seeking services or want to make donations. Make sure the components of your branding are consistent. Key branding elements include these components:

◆ The name of your nonprofit

◆ Your logo

◆ Distinctive use of colors, images, and other graphic elements, used consistently on your website, marketing materials, business cards, stationery, and so on

◆ Your mission statement, slogan, and/or motto

◆ Words and phrases that you use frequently to get the message across

Once you have chosen these elements, then your job is to get the word out to your following so that, in time, everybody in your target audience associates your nonprofit with them—and with your story.

The single most important element of a branding strategy is consistency. That means you must do everything you can to associate your story and your messages with your name, logo, mission, slogans, mottoes, and

---

What do you think of when you see someone wearing a pin in the shape of a pink, knotted ribbon? Most likely you think of two things: breast cancer research and Susan G. Komen.

Susan G. Komen was only thirty-three years old when she was diagnosed with breast cancer, and she died three years later. Her younger sister, Nancy Goodman Brinker, promised her sister that she would do everything she could to end breast cancer, and she founded the Susan G. Komen Breast Cancer Foundation in 1982.

By the twenty-fifth anniversary of the organization, the name was changed to Susan G. Komen for the Cure, at which time they trademarked a new logo, a pink ribbon that resembles a runner in motion. At the time of writing, that pink ribbon shows up on everything from costly jewelry to bumper stickers. During October, Breast Cancer Awareness Month, the Komen shade of pink shows up on everything from yogurt containers to the child-protection caps on prescription containers from the pharmacy!

Komen for the Cure has successfully branded not only its organization, but its *mission:* to end breast cancer forever.

Example

anything else that you think will help people think about your nonprofit, and identify it as a worthwhile charitable investment. Use these phrases, slogans, statements, and images frequently. Repeat them often in all of your marketing messages. Include them in the electronic signature you use in your outbound emails. Frequent use of the branding elements will help to make your nonprofit more visible in a crowded marketing landscape.

To Recap

- ◆ It's up to you to make your target audience aware of you.

- ◆ The work you did to craft your case for support contains the bones of your strategy for public relations and branding.

- ◆ Find and use the keywords and search terms that are likely to attract the right prospects to your site.

- ◆ Build your prospect database through the use of newsletters, blogs, and social media.

- ◆ Constant, consistent attention to your outbound marketing efforts will produce results.

Chapter Seven

Human Resources: Staffing Your Development Program

IN THIS CHAPTER

····→ Development roles and responsibilities

····→ Do you have the right team?

····→ Finding the right people

····→ Making the case for hiring and expanding the development team

The size of your development staff will correlate, to some extent, with the overall size of your agency and the amount of time it's been in existence. The Leaky Bucket study shows that 25 percent of respondents rely solely on the fundraising efforts of the executive director. Of course, this means that the executive director works only part time as a fundraiser and part time as an executive, administrator, manager, program delivery person, and chief cook and bottle-washer. Another 31 percent rely on the executive director plus one other person.

Development is not a job that can be done well in a staff member's spare time. You need to have a dedicated staff person or a team of development people who understand the science and art of fundraising. Development staff needs the right tools to do the job well, so you need to invest in technology, marketing materials, training, and other forms of support.

The development team needs to put in the time required, which is not simply nine to five, and the rest of your nonprofit staff needs to leave them alone to do the work. This chapter will help you develop a budget for development and a plan to hire, train, and retain the best staff people.

Why a Development Office?

At some point in your organization's life, you will need to get serious about fundraising. Even if grants or fees for service fund a large percentage of your programs, eventually these funding sources may change or dry up altogether. To remain in operation and build capacity you will need professional-level fundraising. Establish a development office before you face a serious funding shortfall. That is the best way to ensure your organization's future. Be aware that most development programs take two to three years before they "show a profit."

The Development Office in Your Organization

Establish the importance of the development office within your organization from the very beginning. The chief development officer (CDO) should report directly to the CEO of your organization. The CEO's role in supporting the fundraising efforts of the development office is crucial to success, and the two must work hand in hand in order to show desirable results. The development office must be on an equal level with the heads of the finance office, the program administrators, and the public relations and marketing staff, and it's imperative that development officers have good relationships with these other executives. The CDO should be a part of the management team that runs the organization. It is important for all stakeholders, including external ones such as board, volunteers, and clients, and internal ones such as staff, to understand the importance of the development function in your organization. Your key executives and board members must be aware of and involved in development planning from a strategic perspective. The development office also needs access to the board. The board has important contributions to make in terms of planning and guiding the development function, and it must have feedback showing progress on a regular basis.

Here are a couple of sample organization charts that reflect the importance and value of the development office. One is for a smaller shop and the other, a larger one. Does your structure look anything like either of these? If not, and your development staff is expected to report to another lower-level administrator rather than the CEO, you could be in trouble.

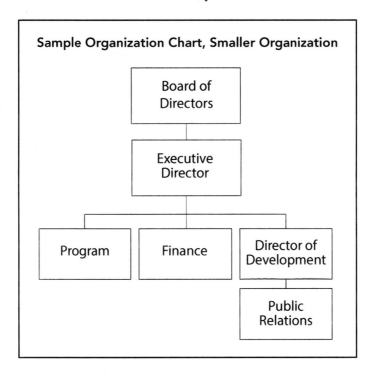

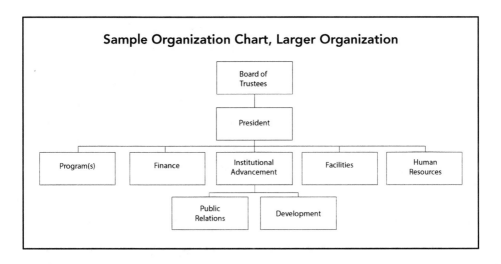

Fundraising Is Everybody's Job!

All staff members need to understand the role of development in your organization and be willing to assist the development office in fulfilling its role. Having the CDO as part of the management team will help ensure that staff understands the role of development and how they can contribute, even if it's just by being enthusiastic. Remember all fundraising efforts must be coordinated through the development office. Other departments should not do their own fundraising without approval and guidance from the development office. You will especially want to avoid having different people from the agency solicit the same prospects for different gifts and programs. Besides the fact that it looks uncoordinated, you might compromise the cultivation of a major gift by pursuing a twenty-five-dollar gift certificate for a door prize at an event. However, the development office can make good use of the contacts, experience, and enthusiasm of program and other staff people.

The CEO's role in fundraising should never be underplayed. Most major donors will want to talk with your CEO when being asked to contribute. Your CEO must be willing to go on solicitation calls, speak to various groups and organizations, and support the efforts of the development staff. A good CEO/CDO team can together lead the efforts to identify, cultivate, and solicit major donors. Your CEO also needs to communicate with the development office about any major changes in the organization, so your development officer doesn't get hit by surprise. Imagine your embarrassment if a development officer is requesting a major gift for a program that your organization is planning to eliminate.

All staff members need to be involved in your fundraising efforts. Members of the program staff can often be your best allies. They might know of potential major donors through the people served by your organization. They will be able to tell the success stories that need to be a part of the case for support. And they are great evangelists, since they understand the programs and know the clients so well.

The finance office needs to understand its role in providing good stewardship of contributions, ensuring that gifts are used the way the donor intended, funds are invested wisely, and reports are accurate. The finance office's role in preparing the annual 990 Form is crucial; fundraising expenses need to be reported accurately. With easy access to financial statements through vehicles such as *Guidestar*, donors can check 990 Forms in the comfort of their homes. The 990 Form can be used as a good public relations tool to promote your organization's programs and services and show good financial health.

Everyone in your organization can help build good donor relations, from the receptionist who answers the phone and connects callers (perhaps major donors) to the right people in a professional and friendly manner to the maintenance or security staff that direct people to the office with a positive attitude. Staff members can assist with events, provide input into grant proposals, and help identify, cultivate, and solicit donors.

Staffing Your Development Program

The size and structure of your development office will vary according to the needs of your organization. Below is a typical organization chart for a medium-sized development office. Compare this with the chart for a large development office on the following page. No matter how large (or small) your development staff is, the same functions will need to be handled by *someone*.

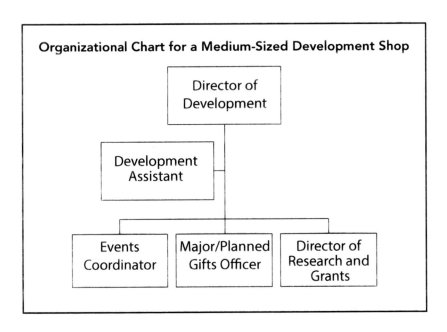

Organizational Chart for a Medium-Sized Development Shop

- Director of Development
  - Development Assistant
  - Events Coordinator
  - Major/Planned Gifts Officer
  - Director of Research and Grants

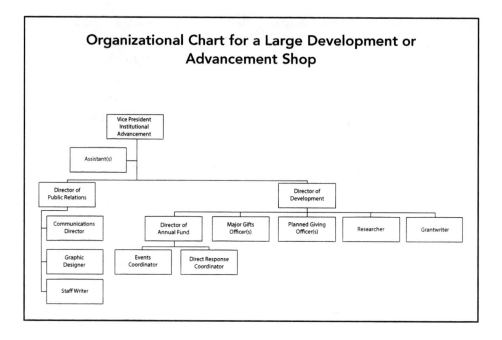

The Chief Development Officer

The title of chief development officer, or CDO, will vary with different organizations. Many universities and colleges use the term "institutional advancement" and the title of vice president for their chief development officer. "Director of development" or "development director" is more common in other types of agencies. Some organizations use the term "resource development" or "fund development" to make it clear that it is a fundraising position. It is important to use a title that will convey to the public and the internal organization that this is an important position and that the chief development officer is part of the management team. The CDO, whatever the title and regardless of the size of the development office, is responsible for directing the following duties:

◆ Researching and identifying potential donors.

◆ Designing and implementing the development plan.

◆ Coordinating all the fundraising activities of the organization.

◆ Working with the board and development committee to implement the development plan.

- ◆ Developing strategies for identifying, cultivating, and soliciting donors.

- ◆ Directing the efforts of volunteers in the development area.

- ◆ Developing appropriate recognition strategies.

- ◆ Educating the organization's staff about ethical and legal issues relating to fundraising.

- ◆ Identifying areas of need to be funded and developing a case for support.

- ◆ Developing appropriate campaign materials to be used for various campaigns and appeals.

- ◆ Holding accountability for the overall performance of the development office.

Often the development office is responsible for public relations. Finding a chief development officer who has the skills to manage all these functions is of utmost importance.

Support Staff

How much staff is needed to support the CDO? The answer will depend in part on the size of your organization, the scope of the job, and the dollar goals that have been established for the development program. If your organization is planning to go "full steam ahead" with a development program, you will need additional staff people to perform tasks such as planned and major giving, research, proposal writing, etc.

You might or might not need to budget for a dedicated support person to manage the donor database. This choice will depend on the type of technology you implement (please see **Chapter Three** for more details). If you use some of the newer, advanced technologies for this purpose, you might not require a full-time specialist to enter data, code it properly, or pull reports. You are more likely to need such a person if you use one of the older but extremely powerful technologies, which are still the preferred choice for many nonprofit organizations and institutions.

In either case, you must budget for adequate training, supportive services, integration or other technical consulting needs, and software upgrades, regardless of the size of your development program. And keep track of who is doing the work. The CDO can easily update a few records in the course of the day but should never spend excessive amounts of time entering tons of data into the system and doing donor research. There won't be enough time left over to build relationships with donors. In order to be effective, the CDO needs to spend time identifying, cultivating, and soliciting the top donors, and should not be spending too much time writing grants, planning events, doing research, and tracking donor records.

A good database manager can be one of the most critical pieces of your development program. This is not a task that can be assigned to a support person with no understanding of development or who lacks the ability to make good judgment calls or understand the importance of accuracy in donor records.

So, How Do We Find Good Development Staff?

In her book, *Fundraising as a Career: What Are You Crazy?* Linda Lysakowski outlines some qualities to look for in a good fundraiser. Develop your "ideal development officer" profile just the same way you would develop your ideal-donor profile: ahead of time. Here's a summary:

Impeccable Integrity

Although integrity is a quality that one either has or doesn't have, there are things you can look for in a development professional that will indicate that the person has integrity. First, does the candidate know, understand, and support the AFP Code of Ethics and Standards of Professional Practice? These documents will provide guidelines about what is ethical in the field of fundraising. Adherence to AFP's Donor Bill of Rights is another key in ensuring that the development staff will hold the donor's interests above its own. Copies of these documents are available from the AFP's website at www.afpnet.org.

Good Listener

Active listening is important to good donor relations. Often a major gift can be secured by a solicitor whose listening skills have been honed. Listening for what the donor's interests are is even more important than being able to persuasively explain the organization's case.

Ability to Motivate

The ability to motivate donors, volunteers, and staff is a critical key for success. Motivating donors does not mean persuading them to do something that they don't want to do or that is not in their best interest. Motivating donors comes through understanding that philanthropy brings joy to the donor and that if the donor really believes in the mission, motivation is simply a tool to bring about the donor's wishes.

Volunteers likewise can be motivated only if your volunteers and fundraising staff share a passion for the mission of your organization.

Motivating the staff of your organization is also important. This starts with having respect and concern for other staff members. Staff members will be motivated by the good example set by your chief development officer. Involving staff members in the development planning process is a good way to motivate them to help implement the plan.

A good practice is to design job descriptions that define results, as well as the activities, programs, and campaigns necessary.

Hard Worker

Development is not a nine-to-five job. Often development professionals are on the job as early as seven in the morning, meeting with volunteers, attending breakfast meetings, or just getting into the office early so they can organize their day before the phones begin to ring and emails start coming in. Likewise, they might easily still be at work at seven or nine in the evening, attending after-hours events, meeting with volunteers, or working at a phonathon. However, working hard does not mean your staff needs to be "wired in" 24/7. Be flexible about comp time and vacations; good development people love to drive themselves to burn-out and beyond, and their managers need to discourage such counter-productive behavior.

Concern for People

If the candidate you're interviewing shows a genuine interest in or passion for your mission and programs, you're off to a good start. If the candidates seem lukewarm, keep interviewing. Good development officers will want to work only for the organizations they're passionate about. They will want to know your clients' stories, understand their hopes and desires, and see how your agency delivers on its promises. With the right attitude and talent, good development professionals will be eager to speak in a compelling fashion about your mission to help build empathy, concern, and market awareness.

Concern for people goes beyond caring for clients and donors; it extends into concern for the staff. Taking time to listen to the concerns of other staff people can help build a concern for people in the development professional. Since so many nonprofit professionals work in emotionally demanding settings, often for low pay, they deserve as much nurturing and support as the clients do.

High Expectations

The best candidates for development staff will hold themselves to a higher standard and will demand the same from their coworkers.

Often it is the development professional that "leads from the middle" and inspires the organization to greatness. Expecting the best from your development staff and other staff within your organization is critical as well. In fact, expecting the best is one of the attributes of great leaders. They simply expect that their followers will live up to expectations, and it works.

Love the Work

Not only do the members of your development staff need to love the organization, but they've also got to love fundraising as well. They come "out of the box" with enthusiasm for raising money and getting to know donors. As with any skill, the more knowledgeable you become in your field, the more likely you'll be to enjoy doing it. Encourage your development staff to learn as much as possible about the profession by taking classes, reading books, attending workshops, and seeking CFRE or other certification.

High Energy

Loving the work will also help your development professionals have the high energy needed to work long hours; motivate donors, volunteers and staff; and meet the expectations the development professional has set or *others* have set.

Perseverance

Perseverance is one of the most highly valued qualities of successful development professionals. Virtually all fundraising initiatives, major and planned gifts in particular, require the building of long-term relationships. Sometimes it takes years for these relationships to pay off. The development professional who keeps great morale over time will deliver better results and feel better about it.

If your development office needs to undergo a major computer conversion, perseverance is definitely going to be required!

Presence

Woody Allen once said, "The biggest contributor to success is showing up." Presence may be the hardest quality to define and cultivate in a development professional. But it's more than just showing up. Maybe we should call it poise or demeanor. A more contemporary definition may be closer to positioning oneself. Presence can be described as the ability to command attention and earn respect as a professional. Carry yourself to command attention.

Your staff should look and act professional at all times. Development professionals, especially when meeting with donors or potential donors, should dress the part. Although that look may vary slightly in different parts of the country, it's always best to err on the side of formality. Wear suits, jackets, dresses; avoid blue jeans and sneakers (unless you're out building a house or cleaning up a shoreline). Being well dressed and well groomed will give the development professional a sense of pride and confidence that is necessary for a sense of presence.

Of course, presence is about much more than just looking good. Development professionals can add to their presence by being experts on your organization, the profession of development, leadership, management, nonprofit strategy. It will also help if your development officers publish books or articles, blog on your website, and participate in appropriate trade associations. Such efforts will make your development officers look and feel more confident.

Setting Goals for Your Staff

Setting goals for your first year of operation is not an easy task, but it's also not as hard as it might seem. Set plenty of nonfinancial goals, especially if there has not been a development program in the past. Your goals may include items such as increasing the size of your prospect database, adopting or refining your donor database system, creating or updating the case for support, setting up an e-newsletter, preparing an online donations page, and setting up the annual appeal or other campaigns.

When establishing financial goals, include subsidiary measurements such as number of new prospects in the pipeline, number of total donors per funding category, and so on. When establishing your financial targets, do not set your goal based on the organization's deficit alone. A realistic assessment of development program expectations is crucial, and some questions must be answered in order to make this assessment.

You also need to have nonfinancial goals associated with your fundraising performance. Some nonfinancial goals could be:

♦ Increase newsletter publication to monthly.

♦ Improve proportions of funding diversification.

♦ Increase the size of the donor prospect list by 10 percent.

Some Questions to Ask Before You Establish Fundraising Goals

❑ Are there potential donors who have supported our programs in the past?

❑ Is there a good donor database in place?

❑ Is the public aware of our organization, and do we have positive relations with the public?

❑ Is our board involved with fundraising?

❑ Does our CEO share the responsibility for fundraising?

❑ How much time will the CDO actually spend doing fundraising, and how much time may be assigned to other tasks such as public relations, updating the website, etc.?

practical tip

◆ Increase the level of board giving to 100 percent.

◆ Visit three prospective major donors every month.

The Leaky Bucket study shows that the majority of nonprofits studied lack *any* performance targets, either financial or nonfinancial. Instead, these targets are completely ignored or described as preferences that are not documented. Contrary to popular belief, your team will produce *better* performance when it knows what's expected. Establishing and documenting goals and targets is one of the easiest, most effective, and least expensive ways to get better fundraising performance.

Evaluating Success

No matter what the overall goals for the development program are, be sure your organization has effective ways to measure success. Develop tracking and reporting systems similar to those discussed in **Chapter Three**. Establish a reporting system so that your development office can report success to the CEO and board on a monthly basis. Include reports that list goals and objectives for each component of the development plan and results for each objective.

How Many, from Where, and for How Much?

For organizations that are just beginning a development program, one of the most challenging aspects of this procedure is finding the right person(s) to staff the office. How many staff members do we really need, where are we going to find them, and how much should we pay them?

There are so many other questions. Do we hire from within or look for candidates from the outside? What skills and talents do we look for? Is it better to hire from the corporate world, the nonprofit sector, or the public sector? Who manages the development staff? How much should we pay them? What should we expect in the first year? And, of course, the big question: Is it worth the investment?

Hire from Within or from Outside?

Always remember that fund development is a profession. You might be able to find someone in your organization who already has the right skills, talents, and attitude to learn the intricacies of development. But what about the cost of the learning curve? It might be tempting to hire from within, but what happens to fundraising results if you move a good employee, whose position may have been eliminated, into a job that's outside the person's experience or preferences? It usually takes a few years before a development professional is up to full capacity.

If you are setting up the development office for the first time, you're probably better off hiring people with credentials, experience, and talent, even if they come at a slightly higher price. The ramp-up time to good performance will be shorter. In other words, think about hiring your CDO *first* and adding more people to the team later. Try to avoid moving a current staff person into the CDO position if the person lacks fundraising skills and experience. The staffer's learning curve might prevent acceptable performance for too long.

So, rather than trying to fit the job into the person's capabilities, the job description should be created first, and it must be aligned with your strategic plan and development objectives. Your organization should develop a job description based on desired results and a set of expectations for the position and then look for the best possible candidate. If there is a current staff person who fills the bill, more power to you, but you must have evidence and confidence that the director of programs is really a director of development in disguise. If not, then you need to look outside—either by placing ads in the right places. (Your local AFP chapter or CharityChannel would be a good place to start.) Or you might want to engage the services of a search firm.

What Skills and Talents Do We Look For?

We've shared some of the many skills and talents that good development people seem to share in common. Remember that skills can be learned and acquired. Attitude and talent cannot. Some less tangible things are more important than technical skills. And passion for the mission of the organization is a must!

Hire from Corporate World, Nonprofit, or Public Sector?

Some advantages of hiring from within the nonprofit sector is that your development officer will already understand how to work with boards—and what it means to work in a nonprofit rather than a commercial business—and will come equipped with a dedication to the mission. On

Information on Salaries

AFP's Compensation and Benefits Survey provides information on annual professional income by years of experience, gender, certification status, type of organization, and position. The complete survey is available free to AFP members in the Member Gateway section of the website. (Note: members will be required to log in.) Nonmembers may purchase the report for a fee by contacting profadv@afpnet.org.

Many organizations offer web-based information on salaries. The Association for Healthcare Philanthropy (www.ahp.org) provides salary surveys and articles for a fee. Other organizations, including Action Without Borders (www.idealist.org) and Abbott, Langer & Associates Inc. (www.abbott-langer.com), provide information free of charge. The Council on Foundations (www.cof.org) provides web-based salary information. Information is provided free or for a fee, depending on the detail required.

The Bureau of Labor Statistics (www.bls.gov) publication titled *Occupational Outlook Handbook* also includes salary information.

In addition, periodicals such *The Nonprofit Times* (www.nptimes.com) and the *Chronicle of Philanthropy* (www.philanthropy.com) publish salary information both on the web and in hard-copy format. This information might be available at your local public or university library.

The organizations listed above are only a few of the many that compile salary surveys.

practical tip

the other hand, someone from the corporate world may have a strong business sense that can really help bring organization and order to your development office as well as have community connections. And an individual from the government sector may have a good feel for how to get things done from the political standpoint.

However, don't make the mistake of hiring businesspeople just because "they are good at sales, so of course they will be good at development," or people from government because they have a lot of political connections, or from nonprofits because they may be willing to work cheaper. A good development person will have dedication to the mission, good business skills, and political diplomacy. Weigh the abilities of *all* applicants in light of these questions: Does this person have impeccable integrity? Will the candidate be able to meet *all* the requirements of the job? Is this person willing to learn more about philanthropy and development? Will our donors respond well to this candidate's style?

Once again, think of hiring your CDO first. Once you have a senior person in place with great development skills and experience, you can take the risk of recruiting a salesperson or bureaucrat as long as the right talents and attitudes are present. The CDO can help such candidates through learning the idiosyncrasies of the nonprofit sector.

How Much Should We Pay?

Compensation is always an issue that causes a lot of questions. Some good places to start are checking the AFP Salary Survey to see what typical salaries are for development officers. This study is broken down by geographic areas, types of organizations, and years in the field, as well as position titles. Local United Ways, statewide associations of nonprofits, or nonprofit centers might have specific information on local compensation practices. Talk to other agencies in your community. If your organization is working with a search firm, the firm will help establish a realistic salary structure.

Although compensation specifics depend on many different factors, a good rule of thumb is to budget for a competitive (i.e., reasonably generous) salary. If you underbudget, you'll end up with underqualified underperformers.

What Should We Expect in the First Year?

Do not expect miracles, but do expect to lay a good foundation. In most cases, a new development office will not show "a profit" for at least three years. There is a very good reason for this. It takes time to cultivate relationships with donors and to build an infrastructure that can support a strong development program. Your executive director should sit down with the new development officer and establish realistic goals for the first year, the first quarter, and the first month. Many, if not most, of these goals in year one should relate to the establishment of a reliable, resilient infrastructure, creation of a comprehensive development plan and budget, and documenting of key policies and procedures.

Be sure to have a written plan with goals and objectives that can be measured on a regular basis. Benchmarking is critical. Not all goals should be monetary, especially in the beginning. A goal to visit a certain number of potential major donors in person each month, to increase the size of the board, or to start a development committee are good places to start. If you're not bringing in much money but you *are* cultivating donor prospects and putting gift or grant opportunities into your pipeline, then your plan is showing results.

Is It Worth the Investment?

Remember what we said about development involving more than just money? It is all about building relationships. Don't just look at the dollars in and dollars out, especially in the first year or so. Look at development as a long-term investment in your organization. Is it worth it to pay people to design and implement programs and provide services to the client? The answer, of course, should be yes. Although it costs money to provide programs, your community needs those programs or your organization would not exist. The same thinking should apply to development. Yes, it is going to cost money to raise money, but the adage, "No money, no mission" is a true one.

Establishing the Development Budget

Establishing the development office budget needs to be done by the development officer and the administrative team. It is unrealistic to think that a development program can succeed without investing in the development office. It often takes two to three years for a development office to bring in enough income to cover expenses, but during that time, the office is building crucial relationships and marketing mechanisms. Start-up costs may be substantial, and it may take a while to develop a donor base. Some things that need to be included in your development budget are:

◆ *Personnel:* Staff salaries and benefits usually make up the greatest part of the development office budget.

◆ *Professional development:* It is vital, particularly if your staff is inexperienced, to allocate money in your budget for professional development, such as attendance at seminars and conferences, and continuing education. If your CDO is not currently a CFRE or ACFRE, your organization might want to invest in helping the CDO gain certification.

◆ *Software and equipment:* A good fundraising system can make or break your development program. Prices for licenses to the software range from several hundred to tens of thousands of dollars; some are higher, and some are free. Cost of licenses is only a part of the technology budget; make sure to budget for the hardware, networking technology, maintenance contracts, support, education services, and so on. Don't forget your office systems (word processing, spreadsheet, presentation capabilities) and your accounting needs. Internet capability and a strong web presence are musts for any development office.

◆ *Office furniture:* This also needs to be considered. Since donors will often visit the development office, the organization does not want to appear too frugal. People could get the idea that there are financial difficulties. On the other hand, the development office of a small social service agency should not look like the office of a corporate CEO.

◆ *Dues and publications:* Membership fees for AFP, CharityChannel, local chambers of commerce, and other civic or professional organizations need to be included in the budget. Include a budget item for subscriptions to the *Chronicle of Philanthropy*, Foundation Center directories, research tools like GrantStation, and books about fundraising.

◆ *Office supplies:* Stationery kit (letterhead, envelopes, business cards), all of which are required for all development professionals. You might also need to set up special stationery for different fundraising campaigns and appeals as well as materials for volunteer training, donor filing systems, etc.

◆ *Communications:* Be sure to budget adequate funds for developing brochures, annual report, newsletter, and website.

◆ *Seed money for events:* If special events are part of your development program, you will need to budget seed money, such as deposits on a hotel and an orchestra for a dinner dance, entertainment at events, a deposit on the golf course for a golf tournament, etc.

To Recap

◆ Once you're ready to get serious about fundraising in your organization, you will need to staff your fundraising efforts. Setting up a development office might begin with hiring a part-time staff person or contractor, but you will quickly find out that development is a full-time job.

◆ The title you give your development staff *does* matter, believe us! We've been there! Your chief development officer should report directly to the CEO and be part of the leadership team of your organization.

◆ Invest in your development office and your staff. It really does take money to make money.

◆ Finding the right staff is critical. Remember that the development officer's primary role is to build relationships between donors and your organization. Having a passion for your mission should be one of the main criteria you use to select development staff.

Chapter Eight

Human Resources: The Role of Your Board

IN THIS CHAPTER

---→ The board's governing role

---→ The board's fundraising role

---→ Where the two overlap

---→ The fundraising tool kit for board members

The board's role in fundraising varies tremendously from organization to organization. Some experts say that the board's only job is to raise money, while others say the board should never raise money. What we've observed is that there's tremendous disagreement about the board's role in fundraising, even among members of an individual board. And this leads to unnecessary tensions and conflict between board and staff.

In the Leaky Bucket study, we found some correlation between the size of the nonprofit and the board's fundraising activities; small, grassroots organizations and start-ups are more likely to rely on their board members and executive director to raise money, while larger, more established nonprofits are more likely to have a development staff plus board involvement. We often find, though, that small nonprofits and newer ones tend to have small, ineffective, or inexperienced boards that do not get involved in fundraising, often because they do not recognize it as their responsibility. Only about 24 percent of respondents have a development team and also involve board members in fundraising.

But these simple statistics are only a small part of the story. Here's what we have observed over the years:

◆ Board members agree to raise money but never do so because they hate to ask for money, they're too busy, or whatever excuse comes up.

◆ There is a lack of clarity about what board members should do versus what staff members should do.

◆ Boards lack members with personal affluence, connections with affluent people, or influence in the community.

◆ Boards don't know how to establish their nonprofit's financial objectives.

◆ Boards make ill-informed demands on their development staffs; for example, throwing more events. (Do we hear weeping and wailing out there?)

◆ Boards focus on balance-sheet minutiae, squabble over the cost of office supplies, and find it easy to cut spending, but don't seem willing to invest in important initiatives, proper staffing, or competitive salaries for staff.

◆ Boards fail to look into the future, consider the long-term sustainability of the organization, or take changing market conditions into account.

There are a million ways for boards to go wrong when it comes to fundraising, and a few simple ways to avoid some of the worst offenses. Let's review them now.

Governance: The Board's Primary Job

John Carver, author of *Boards That Make a Difference*, says something we really like. He says that the board's first job is to make sure the organization is worth raising funds for in the first place. How do boards do so? By understanding and exercising their governance role.

He also says something else: the board's job is one of ownership, not of helping. If anyone is helping, then it's the staff that helps the board, not the other way around. In for-profit companies, the board of directors represents the owners of the business and their interests. If you own one share of a publicly traded company, you are an owner of that business, and the board collectively represents your interest and the interests of the other shareholders. Board members of these corporations do not "help" the employees. They do not stuff envelopes or staff the registration table at the annual meeting. They hold the executive staff accountable for protecting their financial interests.

It's not always quite so easy to figure out who "owns" a nonprofit, but it's safe to say that it's owned by the community it serves. The board of directors represents the ownership of this community. If your nonprofit serves starving children, then you as a board member govern the nonprofit *on behalf of those starving children*. If your nonprofit is devoted to preserving the art of silk embroidery, then your board governs the nonprofit on behalf of those interested in silk embroidery. If these board members stuff envelopes or staff tables, they are acting as volunteers, which is just fine. But such tasks are *not* the tasks of governance.

Wikipedia provides a pretty good definition of governance. It says that it "relates to decisions that define expectations, grant power, or verify performance." Governance, or governing, is what governments do, and the board of directors represents the government of your nonprofit. The tasks of governance are leadership tasks: setting direction, establishing goals and objectives, developing policies, providing guidance.

The governing role covers certain issues that are of immense importance in terms of fundraising, including:

◆ *Establishing fundraising goals:* The board is in a great position to assess how much money should be raised overall to sustain the organization or build its capacity, staff up properly, and retain a financial reserve to manage during bad times.

◆ *Promoting healthy levels of funding diversification:* Sometimes the staff is too close to the fundraising forest to see the trees. The board can assess the extent of funding diversification and encourage better balance.

◆ *Monitoring fundraising performance:* This means having enough insight to know if development efforts are focused on the strategic plan and its objectives. This is an oversight role, not a punitive one. Depending on outcomes, board members might even suggest lowering the targets, for example, during bad economic times.

◆ *Offering guidance on funding priorities:* The establishment of funding priorities is a core governance issue. It's one of the jobs of the leadership. Should we buy a building? What should we do about this underperforming program? Is our staff large enough and skilled enough to meet the challenge, or should we allocate more money for payroll and hire more effective staff?

These decisions should not be made by staff members without input from the board.

Make sure you set some policies in place that empower the board to fulfill its governing role in the area of fundraising. Check off the ones that you have in place today.

❑ We have clear, documented fundraising goals that include our target for overall income.

❑ We assess our funding needs and redefine these goals every year.

❑ We evaluate our staff's ability to achieve the mission, and we recommend adjustments to the staffing plan every year.

❑ We review fundraising performance against our plan at least once a month to ensure that we are staying focused and on track.

❑ If fundraising performance is below targets, the board reassesses our ability to achieve our mission but avoids making tactical demands or undue cuts in expenditures.

The Board's Fundraising Role

Board members may also contribute directly to the fundraising effort. They can leverage their personal and business connections, and they can act as peer solicitors.

It is certainly desirable to have board members take on tasks like these, and it might even be necessary, but it's not part of their governing role. You need to understand that, and they need to understand that.

Leveraging the Board's Connections

Board members are often business owners, community leaders, or major donors to your organization. Even if your board members are not the "movers and shakers" in your community, they *do* know people.

It's desirable to recruit board members with sizable networks of contacts. It's particularly desirable that at least some of your board members have relationships with people who can make a difference on behalf of the organization by exerting influence, bringing attention to your work, volunteering, and donating money, goods, or services.

Fundraising is not governance. Governance is not fundraising. If the board decides to participate in fundraising, then it has agreed to take on an optional task (optional in terms of governance, not optional in terms of raising money). You and your board are well advised to wrestle with this issue and come to a clear understanding about what the board members are going to do, and not do, in terms of raising money.

Finally, make sure that your board members have a genuine passion for your mission. Since board service implies a large investment of time and effort, board members should think of your nonprofit as one of their major philanthropic investments and, therefore, have a desire to promote the organization.

Encourage the board to talk about the value of using its own contacts to spread the word about your nonprofit.

Once the board members have agreed to share their connections, make it easy for them to do so. Many groups have tried to do this by handing out index cards at a board meeting, so board members can write down the names and contact information of two or three people they're willing to approach. In most cases, this is not successful because board members have difficulty coming up with names on the spot. A better method is to

Not too long ago, one of us worked with a nonprofit that had always been funded by a large government appropriation. In the tenth year of its existence, the organization asked the consultant to advise it on establishing a fundraising organization and diversifying its income streams. Since the organization did not have a database of contacts (other than clients), the consultant suggested that the group ask its board members for introductions to their business or personal contacts in the community.

After two or three weeks, the consultant asked the CEO how many leads had been provided by the board members, and he said "none." Turns out that the board members refused to make any introductions! They said several versions of "how can I trust you not to mess up my relationship with these people?" Then they chastised the CEO, demanding to know why he wasn't producing more income.

Moral of this story: Make sure board members understand why you need their help, what it means, and how to do it. If they flatly refuse to leverage their connections, you might have a bigger problem on your hands.

 stories from the real world

give them a simple form that captures name and contact information, a check box or two where the board members can show when they'll reach out to the contact, and so on. You'll find a sample template in **Appendix A**.

Setting up structures and guidelines ahead of time will make the job of leveraging board connections easier. Here's how:

❑ Make sure board members understand why they're being asked to leverage their connections. If they are suspicious, clarify. If they don't come back with any names, ask why. If they really have no such contacts, rethink the makeup of your board.

❑ Provide mechanisms that make it easy for board members to provide the information you need.

❑ Your list of contacts is one of your most valuable fundraising assets. Capture any and all such possible connections in one place, add them to your contact database, and make every effort to keep it up to date.

Peer Solicitation: A Team Sport

Soliciting charitable donations is a professional activity in which board members may participate—*if they choose to do so.* Don't make the assumption that just because these folks sit on your board, they're just dying to go out and raise money for you. It's best that you all agree on the rules of the fundraising game up front, ahead of time. This is why having clear expectations about fundraising in the board position description, and sharing that expectation in the board recruitment process, is critical.

Some board members may be very happy to cultivate relationships but don't want to actually make the ask. Some people just plain hate asking for money, and some donors don't want to be asked by their friends and relatives. Make sure that board members get proper support from the professional staff whenever possible, which can range from preparation to accompanying the board member on the prospect visit.

Board members should focus their efforts on major gifts. Depending on the nonprofit, a major gift can be as small as $1,000 or even less, but it usually means $25,000 or more. Asking board members to invest personal time and energy on smaller gifts is simply not a very good return on their effort.

By contrast, the efforts that produce small gifts, like the annual appeal, the gala, or online donations, are best handled by paid staff members. These strategies produce enormous amounts of income throughout the nonprofit sector, but they require dedicated concentration, skills, and technology support to be successful. Don't expect, or even ask, your board to run such campaigns.

The same goes double for grants-based funding, especially when you're seeking grants from large foundations or government agencies. Board members might have useful connections within foundations, and sometimes the major donor's money comes out of a family foundation, so this is an area where board members can be helpful making contacts. But please recognize that selecting and pursuing grant opportunities is another professional activity and is quite labor intensive. It is not handled particularly well by board members. The rare exception is when the agency is still in the start-up phase and you find a board member with grantwriting experience who's willing to volunteer the time needed.

Establish peer-solicitation guidelines before you expect much in the way of performance. Here's what we recommend:

- ❑ Identify board members who are willing to participate in peer-solicitation efforts.

- ❑ Prepare them ahead of time.

- ❑ Always send a two-person team to make the ask.

The Fundraising Tool Kit: Removing the Guesswork

It always surprises us to find nonprofit organizations that lack the basics of a fundraising tool kit. Remember, we found out that only 22 percent of respondents to the Leaky Bucket study said that they even *had* an up-to-date case statement. If you haven't provided a tool kit to support the fundraising effort, you're setting yourself, your development team, and your board volunteers up for failure.

The fundraising tool kit consists of seven critical components:

1. *The comprehensive development plan:* The development plan is a subset of the strategic plan, and as such, it is part of the board's governing role. Once the plan has been documented, any board members involved in peer solicitation should have a copy of it.

2. *The case for support:* Sorry to beat you over the head about this one. The case for support contains your story, testimonials, anecdotes, funding priorities, how you use your income, naming opportunities, giving levels, and all that useful stuff. If you don't have an up-to-date case statement, go back to **Chapter Four**. Do not pass "Go," and do not collect $200.

3. *Presentation templates:* Put together a standard presentation template to be used when making the ask. It should include standard information plus other stuff that's unique to the particular prospect and opportunity.

4. *Solicitation script:* This is a series of talking points and suggested probing questions, not an actual script that you read to the prospect. Good probing questions tend to elicit a great deal of information quickly—to figure out whether the prospect justifies

additional effort. The prospect might look like a good fit but on further discovery just doesn't make the grade.

5. *Donor-tracking method:* If board members are cultivating donor prospects, they need consistent ways to keep track of what's going on. Create a simple spreadsheet or even a paper and pencil form to get started, but eventually you'll need to invest in a donor-management system. Agree ahead of time on the data you need to capture, track, and report on.

6. *Staff support for peer solicitation*: Make it clear which staff members will support board members in the peer-solicitation effort. Establish a routine for the peer solicitor to keep the staff member informed.

7. *Fundraising calendar:* At the beginning of every year, preschedule critical fundraising dates, including any major events you intend to hold, the dates of major holidays, and any other dates that are important to the fundraising effort. We suggest that you also preschedule all reviews of fundraising performance against your plan. Your calendar should include the estimated dates for running major marketing campaigns, including the annual appeal. This improves coordination between peer solicitors and staff.

To Recap

◆ The board's role in fundraising is critical, but it's equally important that you and your board specify exactly what that role includes and how to fulfill it.

◆ Clarify fundraising expectations for the board. This will contribute to fundraising productivity and go a long way toward establishing harmonious relations between board and staff.

◆ Board governance includes three major fundraising issues: establishing the income targets required to operate the nonprofit at the desired level of capacity, monitoring performance to maintain accountability and stay focused, and providing guidance in setting funding priorities. These three tasks are important for every nonprofit, yet they tend to be underemphasized and misunderstood.

◆ The board can also contribute to raising money by leveraging its connections. And, finally, board members should be encouraged to become peer solicitors by cultivating donor prospects and even making the ask. This work is best conducted in partnership with staff members wherever possible. If some of your board members lack the skills or confidence to solicit, respect their position; if they can make an introduction for you, that's enough.

◆ And don't forget your fundraising tool kit. The elements of the tool kit are your arsenal. They maintain focus and consistency of message (part of your branding strategy). Failing to provide such a tool kit means your board members have to reinvent the wheel time after time. Get it done now!

Chapter Nine

Involving Volunteers in Your Development Program

IN THIS CHAPTER

···→ What roles can volunteers play in our development program?

···→ Where do we find volunteers?

···→ What do volunteers need to succeed?

Although we did not collect data on volunteer fundraising in the Leaky Bucket study, we can share some of our observations about problems and challenges in this area. Once again, we see a relative lack of criteria for recruiting the right volunteers for this role as well as a relative lack of performance targets and expectations for accountability.

One thing that often prevents organizations from involving volunteers is that the board hires a development staff person and then breathes a collective sigh of relief. "Whew, we don't have to worry about that fundraising stuff anymore; the development person will handle all that." So the result is that the CEO and board think that hiring staff is the magic bullet.

Another thing we've seen is that nonprofits tend to think volunteerism means the good folks who will staff our gift shop, mentor the youth we serve, build houses, clean up the river, etc. But *fundraising*—why would volunteers want to do that?

Or "We could use some help with our fundraising, but what would we have volunteers do, and where will we find them?"

A good volunteer base is important for the development office. Volunteers, similar to board members, are often great sources for identifying, cultivating, and soliciting donors. Volunteers usually have more connections with businesses, affluent individuals, and others, than members of your staff may have. Volunteers can approach the "ask" precisely because they are not paid employees. They can share their own commitment to the organization. Volunteers can also be asked to help with specific areas of expertise, such as planned giving, public relations, or strategic planning.

Volunteer Fundraising the Right Way

So, you're in a small development shop, trying to manage grantseeking, coordinate special events, build your major-giving program, and start a planned-giving program, all while maintaining a strong annual fund. How do you keep all the balls in the air and show the results your executive director and board are asking for (or demanding!)? You'd love to hire more staff, but your budget does not allow for any staff increases. Wouldn't it be great to have some "unpaid staff?"

Building a good volunteer base is one way to meet the growing demands of your development office. No, volunteers will not replace staff, but they can be a terrific source of added person power. There are also some distinct advantages to having volunteers involved with your development program even if you have an adequate staff. As we've indicated, volunteers can bring to the table time, talent, and treasure that often the staff alone cannot provide.

The Development Committee

A good place to start involving volunteers is your development committee. The development committee can be an important part of setting up your development program. While in many organizations the development committee consists only of board members, this is one place where it's wise for board members to recruit other people. These individuals will know that they are not being asked to sit on the board itself. Their responsibilities, and their authority, are limited to committee work so they can focus their full energy on development.

This committee can help you create and implement the development plan, assist with opening doors to potential donors, and even help solicit gifts. The development committee should invite several board members to serve and be chaired by a board member, but it should draw the majority of its members from outside the board. This will help your organization expand its fundraising efforts and cultivate potential board members. A development committee of fifteen or more members will provide the skills and talents your organization needs. The committee should be divided into subcommittees such as a planned giving committee, event committees, annual fund committee, etc.

Other Ways to Involve Volunteers in Fundraising

The ARC, formerly known as the Association of Retarded Citizens, is a national organization providing a wide range of services to people with intellectual and developmental disabilities. A local ARC chapter has formed a special committee called "The ARC Angels." These people get together to do everything possible to help the local ARC achieve its mission, with a special emphasis on raising money.

The name is catchy, the members of the ARC Angels are especially proud of their work, and the development office needs fewer staff members to get the job done.

 stories from the real world

Volunteers can help with just about any aspect of your development program. Among the roles they can assist with are:

- ❑ Research
- ❑ Writing
- ❑ Donor stewardship
- ❑ Donor cultivation
- ❑ Direct mail
- ❑ Internet fundraising
- ❑ Telephone fundraising
- ❑ Major gifts
- ❑ Capital campaigns
- ❑ Planned giving

You might currently involve volunteers in some of these areas, but think about expanding these volunteer roles. It is a proven fact that most volunteers want meaningful work and not just "envelope stuffing." Not that you can't ask volunteers to stuff envelopes, but providing more meaningful work tends to keep them more involved for a longer time, and it deepens their commitment to your organization. Here are some ideas you might not have thought about. We invite you to try one or two of these ideas this year and see what a difference it makes.

Research

Invite a group of community leaders to work on a "screening and rating" session to help you identify major donor prospects, assess the prospective donors' ability to give, and determine the best contact to make "the ask" to these donors. Or invite a volunteer who loves searching the Internet to help you find potential foundation funders.

Writing

In most cases, writing grants, fundraising materials, and annual appeal letters is best done by staff or contractors, but if you find volunteers who are top-notch writers, such as retired development professionals, you could invite them to help with writing stories for your newsletter, appeal letters, website pages, or even grant proposals. Just make sure to recruit volunteers who are more than good writers and who also understand development.

Donor Stewardship

Bring together a team of volunteers, including board members, to conduct a thank-a-thon to call donors. You can start with the top 10 percent of your donors, or those you've classified as major donors, and then if you have enough volunteers, move down the list to mid-level or new donors.

Donor Cultivation

Why not ask some of your former board members or major donors who have a passion for your organization to host a cocktail party in their home, a breakfast meeting at your facility, or a luncheon in a restaurant and invite some of their friends whom they believe would also have an interest in your organization? Do not ask for money at these events but rather use them to get acquainted and to build relationships with future donors.

Direct Mail

Ask a team of people who know your community well to review your mailing list and help you update any names on it that might not be accurate. These volunteers will probably know who is deceased, married, divorced, moved away, etc. They could even help you correct errors in your mailing list that would turn off prospective donors who might receive a mailing with incorrect information. And don't forget, every returned piece of mail costs you twice the postage—once to get it sent and returned, a second time to send it to the correct address.

Internet Fundraising

Form a subcommittee of Internet-savvy volunteers who are active in social media and ask them to start a discussion group about your organization that they can tweet, text, and/or post on Facebook.

Telephone Fundraising

If you have thousands of names to call, you'd be wise to engage a telephone fundraising firm, but if you have fewer than a thousand donors, members, or users of your services, you can plan a volunteer phonathon.

Major Gifts

Review the top 5–10 percent of your donors, and invite those donors to volunteer by serving on a special committee that will identify and invite others to be major donors.

Capital Campaigns

If you're thinking about a capital campaign in the near future, invite a small group of people who have served on other capital campaigns in your community to act as a steering committee for your precampaign planning phase.

Planned Giving

Invite a group of allied professionals (CPAs, estate planning attorneys, financial planners, trust officers, and the like) to serve on your planned giving committee. These volunteers can help you by writing articles for your website and newsletter, conducting planned-giving seminars, and identifying potential planned givers for your organization.

Recruiting Volunteers

Recruiting members of your development committee or other fundraising volunteers should follow the same process as board recruitment. Assess your needs, develop the appropriate position descriptions, and then find the appropriate persons to serve on this committee. Some potential members for the development committee might be past board members who want to stay involved in your organization's fundraising activities, those who have volunteered at events, donors, chamber of commerce members, and graduates of leadership programs. You might also want to enlist the help of media and public relations people, development officers, and entrepreneurs. These are people who will have the skills and talents your organization needs on its development committee. Just as with recruiting board members, it will be important to have a position description with clear expectations before you recruit new committee members.

A note of caution: In this conversation about volunteers, we are referring to the volunteers who help you raise money, run the raffle, and plan the gala, not those who build the houses and clean the bird cages. Be careful to differentiate these volunteers from the providers of health care, education, social work, or other professional services who serve as volunteers by donating their professional services. It could be appropriate to expect these doctors, dentists, psychologists, lawyers, and educators to also raise money or do other forms of volunteer work, but this will be an entirely different role. The time and services these professionals donate are already valuable and should be recognized, but often someone with a real passion for your mission might be ready to step up to a new level of volunteer commitment by helping with fundraising.

Identify the right people who meet your needs. The next step is determining who should approach them to extend invitations to serve on the board or development committee or to participate in other fundraising roles. It could be the board chair, development committee chair, a staff member, or another member of the development committee or board. In short, the best person to recruit a board member, development committee member, or fundraising volunteer follows the same rule as determining the best person to ask a major donor for a gift—the person who has the best relationship with them. Often it is a team "ask."

Tips for Recruiting and Working with Fundraising Volunteers

◆ Identify your needs—what is it you want volunteers to do? Work at events, ask for gifts, help with planning, etc.? Make a list of all the ways you could use volunteers in your fundraising activities.

◆ Prepare a job description for every volunteer position, outlining the time that is required, the special skills needed, any expectations for the volunteer's own financial contribution, etc.

◆ Prepare a volunteer recruitment packet that includes the job description, information about your organization, and lists of current board members and other volunteers.

◆ Identify potential volunteers from current donors, past board members, and other volunteers in the organization who are not currently involved in fundraising activities.

◆ Hold a brainstorming session with staff and review the volunteer positions you need filled. You will be amazed at how many connections your staff members have with potential volunteers.

◆ Do the same session with your board and development committee if you have one.

◆ Network, network, network—attend chamber of commerce meetings; visit service and professional clubs. There are often great volunteers just waiting for the right organization to ask them!

◆ Once you've recruited the volunteers, provide them with an orientation session designed to instill in volunteers a passion for your mission.

◆ Provide training appropriate to each volunteer.

◆ Acknowledge and recognize volunteers. Remember that stewardship is important. Let volunteers know how they are making a difference!

practical
tip

Before approaching the prospective volunteer, you need to develop a volunteer-recruitment packet for everyone you are asking to serve in a volunteer capacity. In **Appendix A**, you will find a chart listing some things that should be in those packets.

Volunteer Training

Volunteers and board members often need training in fundraising practice and techniques. Inviting key volunteers to AFP meetings, conferences, and seminars is an inexpensive and effective way to help educate and train volunteers. Another option is to hire a consultant to help train the volunteers. If your budget is tight, ask the senior staff of another nonprofit organization if one of its key volunteers could assist in training yours.

Recruit volunteers for your development committee and other volunteer fundraising positions with a thoughtful, well-planned process, such as the one you use to attract and recruit members of your governing board. Start by determining the skills and connections you will need. Develop the appropriate position descriptions. Then, and *only* then, recruit the volunteers to fill these positions.

Evaluating and Rewarding Volunteers

It's easiest and most effective to evaluate performance when the organization or team being evaluated has clear, documented performance expectations. Encourage the volunteer leadership to establish such performance expectations ahead of time (and give them plenty of guidance and help). Once the plan and schedule have been created, establish regular reviews of performance against plan, with discussions about how to improve results. These regular reviews should take place at least once a month—more frequently if there is a specific campaign that expires soon.

Position descriptions should include term limits, general roles and responsibilities, level and type of desired results, and expectations about the amount of time and financial commitment anticipated or desired.

Your plan should contain ways to reward volunteers, even if the reward itself has no monetary value or cost. A personal thank-you, a pizza party, an announcement in your newsletter; all of these things will be appreciated, but they won't soak up money that would be put to better use elsewhere.

Invite your development committee to make a presentation to the board of directors on the work they have accomplished. Elevating effective development committee members to the board of directors is a good way to recognize their work and commitment.

Among many other things, consider these issues when creating the plan for volunteer performance. Did the committee members get actively involved with the plan? Did they help the organization identify donors? Did they contribute financially and solicit donors? Are there new ventures your organization is considering, such as planned giving, that might require specialized skills on our committee? If so, what could be done to lock in results or even create better ones? If not, what could be done differently to get better results in the future?

So, let's develop a plan to fix what's wrong with your volunteer program by listing ways you can involve volunteers, who you might already have involved in your organization to fill some of these volunteer roles, and where you might find new volunteers.

Volunteer Task	Current Volunteers Who Could Fill This Role	Possible Ways to Recruit Volunteers to Fill This Role

To Recap

◆ Volunteers can play an important role in your fundraising efforts. Whether your organization is small or large, whether you have a mature development program or are just starting out, there are a number of roles volunteers can play in your development office.

◆ There are a number of sources you can use to find and recruit volunteers, but make sure you have first thought out what roles you want volunteers to play and what expectations you have of them.

◆ Once you find volunteers, be sure to provide them with training and the tools they need to succeed.

Chapter Ten

Too Many Eggs, Too Few Baskets: Why Fund Diversification Is So Important

IN THIS CHAPTER

····→ What's wrong with the fund diversification strategy overall

····→ Assessing your current level of funding diversification

····→ Benefits of a diversified fundraising program

····→ Creating fund-diversification targets

Establishing well-balanced diversification of funding streams is no mean feat, but unless you're paying serious and consistent attention to it, you are vulnerable. Any time a single funding source occupies more than a certain proportion of overall income, you're at risk. If that funding source dries up, you can't sustain operations, or at least certain programs, and replacing the lost income always takes longer and feels harder than you expect. Even if you expect the worst, double it.

The Leaky Bucket study shows that about 9 percent of respondents rely on only one or very few funding sources. Considerably more, 25 percent, of the sample rely primarily on a single funding category, usually grants. Half of respondents state that they enjoy a variety of funding sources but that their levels are still not well balanced, while only 16 percent consider their diversification to be well balanced.

That's what the data tells us. Personal observation adds a few more nuances to this issue.

Mature vs. Immature Nonprofits: Who's More Likely to Have Low Levels of Diversification?

The term "organizational maturity" measures more than the number of years a nonprofit has been in existence. It also measures the level of sophistication, documentation, effectiveness, and so forth that characterize the way the nonprofit is run.

Nonprofits might be immature even if they have been in existence for decades; some nonprofits may be organizationally quite mature even if they have only been in business for a few years. And don't forget that an otherwise mature organization could have a development program that is still in its infancy. The Leaky Bucket Assessment measures the level of maturity of nine basic fundraising practices. See **Appendix A** for access to some other methods for assessing your organizational maturity.

Immature nonprofits are much more likely to have low levels of diversification. This is especially true for nonprofits in the social service arena, where we see a heavy reliance on grants-based funding. However, there is a fairly large subset of nonprofit organizations that were launched with the expectation that they would always be funded by a sole source, typically a government or quasi-governmental agency like the state's department of children's services. In both types of organizations, the infrastructure for developing and maintaining diversified funding streams may be absent or weak. As a result, both board and staff tend to assume that diversifying funding is either unnecessary or far less important that simply making sure the major grant or appropriation is renewed.

If you have only one funding source, then you have only have one funding source to lose. If your only funding source is a government agency and the agency needs to cut costs, your nonprofit is at risk. And if that funding source restricts your programs or mission or client base, then you and your leadership team are no longer in charge of delivering on the mission. The funder is.

Underfunding Fundraising: Who's Doing the Work?

As we saw in **Chapter Six**, there is a clear correlation between the maturity of the nonprofit and the number of staff members dedicated to fund development. Organizations with no dedicated fundraising staff are more likely to have low levels of diversification. These nonprofits are more likely to limp from year to year, unsure of whether they'll break even in any year. And obviously, if your nonprofit gets all its income from a single source, why would you have a development person anyway?

When these nonprofits start to worry about diversification, it often seems like an impossible task. There's nobody on the team that has the time or expertise to do the work. So the work (a) goes undone, (b) gets done inconsistently by board members or the executive director, and/or (c) gets done poorly because you've got people without skills, knowledge, or time trying to do the impossible.

Where Are We? Assessing Your Current Levels

Figure out the proportion of funding you obtain from each major fundraising category. We have found that the best insights arise when you consolidate all your income into the fewest categories or streams possible. A good way to do this is to lump together all individual donations into one stream, which of course includes all income from events, auctions, online donations, and the annual appeal. Then do the same with major gifts, income of all kinds from corporate donors and sponsors, grants and appropriations from private foundations and government agencies, and, if it's appropriate, a category that covers fee-for-service income and product sales. If you consolidate your information into a few broad categories, it's easier to see the proportions.

> Adding development staff is just as important as adding program or technical staff. Maybe it's even more important. Don't put it off too long—hire people to do development for you as soon as you possibly can.
>
>
> **important**

Once you've calculated the totals, figure out the percentages represented by each stream. Finally, you can create a pie chart that shows the size of each slice of income.

There are several pie charts in **Appendix A**. First there is a chart showing national average for giving in the United States from individuals, corporations, and foundations. We also include a blank pie chart for you to fill in *your* results. Once you've compared the two, you will have a better idea of which areas you need to work on. The national averages do not take into account government funding and fee-for-service income, but they will give you an idea of how you compare in *philanthropic* giving.

This exercise is extremely helpful in visualizing your current status. You will find blank copies of the table below, and its associated pie-chart template, in **Appendix A**. Bristol Strategy Group, Ellen's company, has also developed an automated Fund-Diversification Calculator that calculates all the percentages and creates your pie chart automatically, and you will find a link to download it, also in **Appendix A**.

Funding Stream	Total Dollars for Current Year	Percentage of Total Income (approximate)
Private foundation grants		
Government grants and appropriations		
Corporate sponsorships		
Corporate donations		
Individual donations		
Earned income		

Where Do We Want to Be? Setting Diversification Targets

Now, decide how you'd like to change proportions in the coming year (or longer). Remember that you simply can't change income proportions dramatically in twelve months or fewer; it can take several years to do so. So if you currently bring in 90 percent of your income from grants, 5 percent from individual donations, and 5 percent from product sales, think about changing to 80 percent grants next year, 10 percent individual donations, 5 percent corporate contributions, and 5 percent product sales (or something like that).

A good rule of thumb is to seek the same dollar amount of money from your major category, while increasing the amount from another category or categories, rather than reducing the amount from the major category.

Enter your income targets in the table below and recalculate the percentages.

Funding Stream	Total Dollars for Current Year	Percentage of Total Income (approximate)
Private foundation grants		
Government grants and appropriations		
Corporate sponsorships		
Corporate donations		
Individual donations		
Earned income		

Again, refer to **Appendix A** for blank copies of the table and the pie-chart template.

Benefits of Diversified Funding

The first and most obvious benefit of good fund diversification is that you're much less vulnerable. If any single funding stream performs poorly, the other streams can keep you going. And if you lose any single funder, the other funders take up the slack.

It's a great idea to set up guidelines for funding, to the point that you can say something like "No single funder will represent more than such-and-such percentage of our total income." With a guideline such as that, you're always making the effort to find new sources and retain current sources so that fundraising produces consistent, predictable, and reliable income.

But there are several other benefits of well-balanced diversification, such as:

◆ *Capacity building*: When you enjoy well-balanced diversification, you enjoy many different fundraising relationships. These different funders can help you build capacity, not just because you'll have more income overall, but because your funders will have a wider set of interests and influences to share with you. With well-balanced diversification, you'll have more unrestricted funds as well as be able to explore more opportunities to fund special projects.

◆ *Innovation:* The broader base of support that comes from diversification also gives you and your leadership exposure to new ideas. Among other things, as you enlarge and diversify your base of support, you'll find yourselves talking to and working with more people and organizations with different perspectives who share a passion for your mission.

◆ *The mentality of abundance:* Too many nonprofit professionals become accustomed to doing with less. Somehow—and pardon our new-age thinking here—when you constantly assume that you can't afford it and you can't make any money fulfilling your mission, you end up with less money, and it's harder and harder to achieve your mission. To the point where you get burned out. When you've got adequate funding, and you're not worrying about where the next payroll is coming from, you become more hopeful, more open to the idea that "there's more where that came from." And that your mission, your nonprofit, and even *you* deserve to have it.

◆ *Freedom from restriction:* As your funding base expands and diversifies, you and your leadership team can really follow your hearts in terms of achieving your mission; you don't have to do this or that—or refrain from doing stuff—just because the funder says so.

◆ *The ability to handle transformational gifts*: From time to time, a successful nonprofit will encounter a so-called transformational gift, typically a gift of such size and impact that the organization can transform itself in a positive way. For example, a long-term donor steps forward and offers to underwrite the building of a new facility, even before anybody breathes the words "capital campaign." If you get such a large gift while your funding is poorly diversified, then your finances become lopsided and you'll have more trouble sustaining the benefits of that large gift. On the other hand, if your funding is already well diversified, you're more likely to be able to tolerate the mixed blessing of a gift so large that it changes your strategic objectives.

◆ *Sustainability:* With well-diversified funding, you're never at risk of closing your doors or cutting programs if any single donor leaves you.

Slow and Steady Wins the Race: Improving Your Fund Diversification

When your funding pie has one or two little teeny-weeny slices and a single big fat slice, you know your funding is not diversified at all and that you're vulnerable as can be. However, it's one thing to draw a picture of a pie that has a nice even bunch of twelve or sixteen or twenty-four slices and quite another thing to do it in practice.

Changing your levels of funding diversification requires consistent attention to the issue over the very long term. There's no time like the present to start this effort, but be realistic over what it takes to get there. After all, different funding streams require different talents, skills, strategies, and support mechanisms to obtain. If your team knows only how to obtain grants, don't expect them to turn around overnight and become experts on major gift work or corporate relations. Also note that it can take a very long time to bring in the first few donations from these new sources.

So set yourself modest but realistic diversification goals starting immediately. Here's a fairly simple approach:

◆ *Start with what's easiest for you.* If you're already good—or
at least experienced—at winning grants, seek to expand the
number of grantors and the overall amount of grants-based
income. If you've already got individual donors, maybe it's time
for major gifts.

◆ *Then explore the next-easiest type of funding.* Do you think your
nonprofit would be appealing to corporate donors or sponsors?
How about individual donors? Are you ready to take on major
donors yet? Before you even try to find these donors, do some
research to figure out which funding category seems like the
next logical step. Don't jump to major-gift work if you've never
gotten any individual donations. Don't solicit huge corporate
sponsorships before you've ever gotten a single company to buy
a table at your gala. Evolve into these new markets. Don't jump
in over your head.

◆ *Build the infrastructure to handle the new category before you
try to raise the money.* Research the category to see whether
these types of funders support nonprofits in your sector or with
similar missions. Interview a few people to find out what they'd
need to see or hear from your nonprofit in order to be interested
in supporting you. Create the marketing materials and other
collateral that will appeal to prospective donors in this category.
If your development staff members don't know how to cultivate
prospects in this category, get them some training, bring in a
consultant, or hire someone who knows how.

◆ *Set achievable targets.* Don't expect to change funding
proportions by more than 5 or 10 percent in the first year
or two. Also set targets for such nonmonetary objectives as
expanding the size of your target database for the new category,
producing collateral materials and outbound campaigns aimed
at the category, and creating a pipeline of opportunities from
prospects in the category.

To Recap

◆ If your funding base is not well diversified, the future of your nonprofit is not particularly well ensured, no matter how meaningful or important your mission may be.

◆ Although you might currently find it easy to manage with just a few funding sources, at some point you're going to hit the wall. You won't have the money you'll need to expand, change direction, add staff, accept more clients, repair or replace aging plant or equipment, and so on. And worst of all, you and your staff are going to burn out and lose heart.

◆ Achieving healthy levels of diversification requires patience, skill, and consistent attention. The good news is that the more you work at it, the easier it gets, and the more skillful your organization becomes at funding itself in a healthy manner.

◆ If you've ever faced significant funding cuts—or even the threat of them—because your government-backed funding is threatened, you know how anxiety provoking this problem can be. If the funders are cutting their funding, you have to cut your budget—unless you've already diversified to the point where reduced support from one source or category doesn't have to compromise your services or direction.

Chapter Eleven

Grants-Based Funding

IN THIS CHAPTER

---→ Why it's so easy to overdo—or underdo—your grants strategy

---→ What you'll need to know to select and pursue the right grant applications

---→ Moving grantsmanship from main base of support to special projects

tatement #9 of the Leaky Bucket Assessment reads, "Check the following techniques that your nonprofit uses when fundraising performance runs below desired levels." The second most popular option so far is "Write more grant applications." In case you've forgotten, the most popular option is "Hold more events." Too bad both of these are risky options. It's not necessarily "bad" to write more grant applications, but the question arises: Are these the right applications? Do they offer more long-term funding? Could your time be better spent cultivating other types of funding sources?

While grantsmanship plays a deservedly strong role in fund development, there are a few ways in which it's easy to mismanage this income stream.

◆ *Fund diversification:* Many agencies rely on grants-based funding almost exclusively. This is most likely to be true for grassroots start-ups and social-service agencies but is certainly not limited to them. And of those agencies with a single source of income, almost all of them get their grant money from a government or quasi-governmental agency, which of course makes the agency vulnerable to government budget cuts.

◆ *Staffing resources:* Agencies that rely on grants-based funding tend to be poorly prepared to tackle other funding sources. If you have a grants expert on your staff, that's great, but the grants person is not always equally expert at developing the annual appeal, setting up individual donor strategies, managing major-gift work, or cultivating corporate relationships. And the appropriate marketing and other mechanisms have not been developed either.

◆ *Long-term retention:* It's not uncommon for a foundation to restrict the number of times an agency can renew its grants. If your organization wins a grant from a foundation that gives for only three years, you've got to start planning to replace that income long before the three-year mark has been reached. And since it costs about six times as much to acquire a new funding source, you can't afford to skimp on this issue.

◆ *The opportunity pipeline:* Because grants typically represent larger chunks of income, it's easy (and tempting) to assume that you need to win only a few of them and, therefore, you have to make only a few applications. For reasons that elude us, this seems to translate into carrying too few grant applications in the opportunity pipeline. Don't let yourself believe you're going to win every grant application you apply for.

◆ *Ignoring granting guidelines and matching requirements:* Foundations typically publicize their granting guidelines (what they'll fund and what they won't, what criteria the applicant needs to meet, and so on) and their matching requirements (the amount of money the nonprofit has to put up in order to win the grant). Inexperienced grantseekers may ignore these guidelines, to their detriment. It takes a long time and a lot of work to complete a grant application, and that work is wasted if you don't meet the basic requirements.

What's *Right* about Grants-based Funding?

There are, in fact, many reasons to have a strong, reliable grants strategy, so let's take a look at the most pertinent of them.

Because That's Where (Some of) the Money Is

Private foundations and some other grantmakers exist in order to give money away, which means they have to have a lot of money in the first place. One of the ways in which foundation executives measure their success lies in how much money they are able to give away and how well their grantees use it.

Because Grantors Help You Get Money from Them

It's in the grantor's best interests to help applicants write good applications and succeed in winning the grants. Remember this; the grantor's staff wants to help you win grants. If you are new to raising money, if you don't know how, or if you're squeamish about it, the grant application process is a great place to start.

Grants Are Great Sources for Funding Special Projects and Initiatives

Let's say you've gotten pretty good at delivering your primary programs and services, and now you see an opportunity to branch out into something new. Rather than trying to pay for it out of your operating budget, seek a grant that will allow you to test the proposition and do the necessary preparation for the opportunity, and then see if the opportunity can be sustained.

The Start-Up Grants Strategy

Let's assume your nonprofit is relatively young, and you're now ready to fund it at a more ambitious level. If you're like many founders of nonprofit start-ups, you have invested your own money and that of friends and family to get up and running, and now your programs are getting more interest. Maybe you run a social-service ministry out of your church or synagogue and it's serving more people than your congregation can easily sponsor. This is the point where young grassroots and start-up organizations are ready to seek their first grants.

Getting the first grant or two usually represents a steep learning curve. First, you have to figure out which grantmaking organizations will finance organizations like yours, at your level of maturity and years in service, and then you have to learn to write the winning grant application.

In fact, your first step is always to document the criteria that the *grantmaker* should meet in order to make it worth your while to apply for the grant. If you're new to grantseeking, criteria like these are the fundamentals:

◆ The funder must provide grants to nonprofits in your geography.

◆ They must support agencies serving the kind of clients you serve, with missions and programs similar to yours.

◆ They must provide grants to organizations as young (or old) as your organization.

◆ Their match requirements must be realistic. If you can't match the amount required through other funding sources, don't pursue the grant.

◆ They must *not* accept grants by invitation only. If you're too young or not well known, you're not going to get those invitations.

◆ Their grants allow the grantseeker to allocate some of the money for administration and overhead.

◆ The grant floor, or minimum amount, must be high enough to make the application worth your time and effort, while the grant ceiling, or maximum, must not be so high that you can't make use of the money without significantly more staff or physical space.

When your organization is in start-up mode, it's likely that grants will play a large part in your funding strategy. There are exceptions to this rule, including arts organizations, especially performing-arts organizations, where a large portion of income stems from ticket sales.

Using grants to launch your agency, or to move it from local start-up to established player, can be a great idea. For one thing, the cost/benefit ratio is relatively favorable. While it may cost you something in time and effort to apply for the grant, every grant you win is usually relatively large, ranging from a low of $1,000 to as much as millions. You can fund a lot of clients and programs and services—even staff—for that amount of money.

But eventually, relying on grants becomes unwieldy and insecure, for reasons we have explored in greater detail in other chapters. Primarily an all-grants strategy represents poor levels of funding diversification, and it cuts you off from other desirable funding sources.

Sometimes grantors are a little bit like banks. They often refuse to grant money to nonprofits that are less than so many years old, just as banks often don't want to lend money to a start-up business because it's an unknown quantity. If you are trying to find grants for a start-up organization, then you must include that fact in your selection criteria. If the grantor doesn't fund start-ups, don't waste your time.

 practical tip

The Special-Projects Grants Strategy

Once your agency can produce a regular flow of income from diverse sources, it's time to think about grants as a way to fund special projects or explore new service opportunities. Such grants can include income for capacity building, preparing for or exploring a new program, and so on.

As important as it is to have a thoughtful strategy for grants-based funding, it is important to recognize that the largest amount of all funding for all nonprofits throughout North America comes from individual donations, somewhere around 80 percent, according to Giving USA.

food for thought

When you engage in such special projects, you'll often find that your board will be more amenable to the idea if you can finance the concept through a grant rather than allocate monies for the project out of your operating budget.

Let's define what is meant by capacity building, a term that is sort of squishy, whose meaning isn't always clear. Capacity building refers to the various tasks and activities designed to make your nonprofit able to handle *more*: more clients, more staff, more or better outcomes, more or better governance, etc. Typically capacity-building projects encompass these kinds of things, each of which is a discrete function that's (relatively) easy to pay for with a grant:

◆ *Planning:* Hiring a consultant to facilitate the development of a strategic plan, business plan, operational plan, or a fund development plan

◆ *Technology:* Purchasing, upgrading, or outsourcing the agency's information or other technology, including consulting advice and/or maintenance services

◆ *Staffing and recruiting services:* Hiring a consultant to evaluate and assess the agency's staffing resources; hiring a recruiter, etc.

◆ *Professional development:* Educational or consulting services to improve leadership and management skills, improve staff credentials, or provide or enhance other technical skills

◆ *Board development:* Educational or consulting services to improve board governance skills or policies, recruit new board members, develop board orientation programs, and the like

Recently, a nonprofit applied for and won a large three-year grant specifically to explore and launch a social-enterprise project. The purpose of this project is to take the agency's internal model of supporting its clients and convert it into a set of services that can be sold to other nonprofits around the country. The grant will be used to conduct a feasibility study, do some market research, document the model, design training programs, and so on. It will pay for outside service providers and a portion of staff salaries. Without the grant, the agency would not have been able to pursue the opportunity since it would not have been able to pay for it out of the operating budget. This is a perfect example of using grant money to underwrite a special project.

stories from the real world

How to Find the Grants You Seek

Before you even seek them out, first figure out which kinds of grantmakers are likely to make grants to your kind of nonprofit, for the purposes you're trying to finance. As always, spend the time to figure out which grants and grantmakers are right for you, before you start making applications. You'll save yourself a ton of money, time, and disappointment if you do.

Start your list of criteria with the fundamentals mentioned above in the section called "The Start-Up Grants Strategy." Now add to it all the other things that will characterize the best possible grantmaker you could ever find. This is where you can and should spell out the qualities and values you find most desirable. So ask yourself questions like these, which go beyond the conventional granting guidelines.

◆ Should your ideal grantor be willing to act as a mentor or planning partner?

◆ How much help and attention do you want them to give you during the application process?

◆ How important is it to the grantor for you to succeed?

◆ How tough are the grantor's reporting requirements, and are you willing to put up with them?

Resources for Finding Grants

Start with the Foundation Directory. A subscription to this directory is usually too costly for smaller nonprofits, so take advantage of it through other means. This online database is usually available at your public library, a local university library, your local community foundation, United Way, or other management-support organization (MSO) that helps nonprofits in your area.

> Most of the time when we're applying for grants, or trying to get a donor to give us a gift, we tend to focus on the question "do these guys think we're good enough for them?" We like to turn that question around and ask "is this prospect good enough for us?" It turns out that once you ask the latter question, you do a better job of finding, and winning, the grants and gifts you seek, and it reduces the anxiety level wonderfully.
>
> **food for thought**

The Foundation Directory allows you to select grantmakers based on a wide variety of search criteria, and the resulting list will include a great deal of information about the grantmaking organization, contact information, including emails, and many other details that will help you decide whether or not to follow up on the foundation.

There are other online resources for finding grants and grantmakers. Make sure you look for them. Also, make sure you get on the mailing lists of the major grantors in your area, including the local or state grantmaking agencies that fund your type of nonprofit. These organizations will not only publicize their funding cycles and grantseeking opportunities, they will also tell you lots of other valuable information that will help you gain expertise in navigating around the local grantmaking community.

To Recap

◆ Grants play an important role in nonprofit funding.

◆ It's up to you to understand when to seek grants, and for what purpose. It's also up to you to raise your likelihood of winning the grants you seek! Understand which grants and grantmaking organizations are right for you, where your chances of winning the grant are better than even, so it's worth the time and effort to pursue it.

◆ While many young and start-up nonprofits might rely almost exclusively on grants to fund their operations, it's advisable to move to a more diversified funding strategy as soon as possible. Around 80 percent of all nonprofit funding comes from individual donations.

◆ Use grants funding for special purposes such as capacity building.

Chapter Twelve

Special Events

IN THIS CHAPTER

····→ Which events are right for our organization?

····→ How do we convince our board that adding another event might not be the answer to eliminating our deficit?

····→ Can we run events with a volunteer committee?

Walks, runs, galas, golf tournaments, rubber ducky races—what are these events all about, how do you run one, and which one is right for your organization? How many events should you run each year? All of these questions are faced by most nonprofits at one time or another.

Statement #9 of the Leaky Bucket studies practices used when fundraising performance runs below desired levels. A high percentage of respondents (49 percent) said that their agencies "increased the number of fundraising events." We were not able to record all the moaning and groaning heard once the development folks found out about that statistic.

There are several reasons that special events are popular fundraisers for nonprofits:

◆ Almost any organization can run a special event.

◆ The money raised from events can go into unrestricted operating costs of your organization, since most event attendees don't expect that their event money will go to fund a particular program.

◆ Events are a good way to raise awareness of your organization.

On the other hand, there are some compelling reasons *not* to hold events:

◆ They are very labor intensive for the staff.

◆ Donors and volunteers can get burned out by attending and working at events.

◆ Events can lose money if not run properly.

◆ There is a great deal of competition for events; the established "big events" will always outperform the first-time luncheon of the new kid on the block.

Finally, your board of directors might encourage holding more events because they can't think of anything else that will close the funding gap. It's important for nonprofit executives to gently dissuade the board when its desire for an event is not the appropriate solution. You will find it easier to do so when you have the evidence—the data—to make your case effectively.

Some typical events run by nonprofits include:

"Thons"

◆ Walkathons

◆ Marathons

◆ Dance-A-Thons

◆ Bike-A-Thons

◆ Bowl-A-Thons

◆ Etc.

Dinners and Dinner Dances

◆ Galas

◆ Award dinners

◆ Testimonial dinners

◆ Roasts

Sports Events

◆ Golf tournaments

◆ Tennis tournaments

◆ Etc.

Auctions

♦ Silent auctions

♦ Online auctions

♦ Live auctions

Other Events

♦ Festivals

♦ Health fairs

♦ Wine-tasting events

♦ Rodeos

♦ Concerts

♦ Office Olympics

♦ Horse, pig, balloon, hospital bed, or auto races

♦ And many more, including one of our favorites, "cow chip bingo!"

Tips for Successful Special Events

One thing that makes a big difference in the success or failure of your event is the planning of the event. You will need to think carefully about some of the factors that go into the event planning before you choose the best event for your organization.

Volunteer Committees

You will want to involve a volunteer committee to help you plan and implement the event. The size of the committee will vary depending on your event. Events might involve a committee of ten, a hundred, or more volunteers. For example, a golf tournament generally has a chair and a few committee members who will secure prizes for the tournament, a publicity chair, a facilities chair who will work on the arrangements with the golf course, a refreshment chair, a subcommittee to recruit foursomes to play in the tournament, and a sponsorship subcommittee. On the other hand, a block party that runs for several days or a week might have hundreds of volunteers working at the booths in two- or three-hour shifts.

Questions to ask before you plan an event:

❑ What do you want to get out of the event? Money, connections, press coverage, or all of the above?

❑ Do you have enough volunteers who are enthused about this event?

❑ Will your board support the event?

❑ Does your development staff have time to manage all the details of the event without compromising other fundraising activities?

❑ How many other organizations in your community are doing similar events, and when are they scheduled?

❑ Is this event something your constituents will support?

❑ How much "seed money" is needed to fund the event start-up?

❑ How much can you reasonably expect to net from this event?

❑ What are the total costs to run the event, including staff time?

❑ Do you have sufficient time to plan the event and bring in a large enough audience?

❑ Does this event fit the mission of your organization?

!
important

No matter what type of event you have, there are a few things to keep in mind about working with volunteers on special events:

◆ Make sure volunteers are aware of the goals of the events (i.e., is this a fundraising event or a friend-raising event?) If it is a fundraising event, what are the dollar goals? If a friend-raiser, what is the goal for the number of people attending, and what information do you want participants to receive?

◆ Every volunteer must have a job description outlining the expectations for the job and the timeframe involved.

◆ Committee chairs and/or staff volunteer coordinators should have methods for holding volunteers accountable to make sure everything gets done on time.

◆ You must provide volunteers with the tools they need to do their job (special training, staff support such as handling registration, or special technology to make their job easier).

◆ Volunteers should be carefully matched to the skill set required for this event. For example, if the event requires an emcee, do you have a volunteer who is experienced and comfortable with public speaking?

Board Support

Another critical factor in deciding which events you will run is the level of support that can be expected from your board. For example, if you are planning a black-tie gala dinner dance in a posh hotel, do you have board members who can afford to attend, and will they sell tickets to their friends? Events such as award dinners, dinners with silent auctions, etc., can be very effective, but people will notice if your board members are not in attendance. Board members should be willing to host tables, get foursomes to play golf, sponsor bowling teams, etc. If they are not committed to the event, you may want to find an event that is more likely to be supported by your board.

Staff Time

No matter how dedicated and enthusiastic your volunteers and board are about the event, your staff will almost always need to devote a great deal of time to managing the event (and the volunteers). Staff will be needed to handle registration for the event, mail out invitations, sort and store prizes, etc. One thing to keep in mind is how much time this event will take away from other tasks

Before embarking on an event, you must know how many volunteers will be needed, what types of volunteers, and whether you can reasonably expect to recruit a sufficient number of volunteers with the skills needed to implement this event.

important

that staff could or should be doing. Often, the *opportunity costs* make an event not worth the time and trouble, even if it is financially profitable. Remember the opportunity costs and the dollar amount you've determined is the cost of your fundraising time (see **Chapter One**). Be sure you have adequate staff before launching a special event. There is a special event analysis form in **Appendix A** that helps you determine not only the staff and volunteer time involved in this event but other factors as well, such as "Does this event help us build relationships with major donors?"

Competition

Many communities have dinner dances and golf tournaments every week, and your community can get burned out by too many of such events. Even if you come up with a novel idea for an event, after a few years, especially if it is extremely successful, other agencies might "borrow" the idea. Before planning an event, you should investigate who else in your community is doing similar events, how long they have been doing them, and what their track records are for successful events.

You should also look at the timing. Are there other competing events on the same day or week you are planning yours? Sometimes you can join forces with other organizations to have one large event (more about this under "A Word about Collaborative and Third-Party Events.")

One of us was approached for advice by two board members of a start-up organization. They wanted to host a black-tie gala at the Four Seasons. When the consultant asked them how many tables they felt their board would be able to sell, they said, "Oh, our board can't afford to attend this event." The consultant's next question, "Well, who *do* you think will attend this event?" was met with blank stares. Finally one of them spoke up and said, "Yes, but ABC Organization (a well-established organization in the community with a power board) has an event like this, and they make lots of money at it." Needless to say, they did not hold the event. But until they were asked these questions, they actually thought they could pull off the event with no idea of who would purchase tickets.

stories from the real world

Community Support

One of the main considerations is whether or not the community will support this event. If your business donors feel there are too many galas, golf tournaments, runs, etc., already, they might not want to sponsor one more. Some companies have established guidelines that prohibit sponsorship of all events or certain types of events. Ask some of your donors and board members if the companies they work for would sponsor this event. Some communities are feeling too tapped out when it comes to events and might limit the number of events they will sponsor or attend annually. Survey your constituents before you decide on the event.

The Event Budget

Once you decide on the event you want to hold, you must develop a budget for both income and expense, and you must be certain that committee members, staff, board, and volunteers are all aware of the budget. Some things a typical event budget might include are:

Income	Cash	In Kind
Ticket sales		
Sponsorships		
Auxiliary income (auction, raffle, sale of goods, etc.)		
Gross revenues		
Expenses:		
Facility rental		
Music		
Food and beverage		
Raffle prizes		
Publicity		
Audio/visual		
Invitations printing/mailing		
Decorations/flowers		
Photography		
Speaker fees		
Insurance		
Fees, licenses, permits		
Staff time		
Total expenses		
Net revenue		

Planning Time

It is also critical to make sure that you allow enough time to plan the event. Most events take about a year to plan, and usually the planning for next year's event starts with the debriefing after the current year's event. Some facilities need to be reserved well in advance, and if you have special entertainment or guest speakers, it might be necessary to book, and pay a deposit, well in advance of your event. You will want to have a cochair of the event who will take over the chair position the following year so that event planning will be seamless.

It is important to understand the difference between gross revenues and net revenues. Many people look at the money taken in at the event and forget to deduct the hard and soft costs of running the event. A typical event generally *nets* about 50 percent of the *gross* income. But often when organizations talk about how much they made at an event, they cite *gross income*. What you really need to look at is *net income*.

important

Mission-Related Events

The most successful events are those that are closely related to your mission. For example, the local 4H Club could be very successful with a Kiss a Pig Contest or Cow Chip Bingo. Patrons of the local art museum, however, would not be likely to relate to this type of event but would probably enjoy a gala dinner in the art galleries of the museum.

Before deciding on an event, think about how well it relates to your mission: Will it help attract the people who are likely to be donors to your organization, and will it persuade people of the value of your organization's mission?

Choosing the Right Event for Your Organization

So, how do you find the right event for your organization? Ask yourself the following questions:

◆ Does this event fit with and promote our mission?

◆ How much can we expect to raise?

- How much do we need to spend?

- Do we have volunteers who know anything about running an event like this?

- Will our board members attend, sell tickets, and sponsor the event?

- How much staff time is involved, and do we have a staff person with the skills to manage the event?

- Will this event help us raise community awareness of our organization?

- Will our donors and friends support this event?

- What risks does this event have, and are we prepared to handle that risk?

Pitfalls of Special Events

Some things to think about before deciding on your event:

- Is this event likely to be adversely affected by bad weather (an outdoor concert, for instance)?

- Can you insure against losses at the event (i.e., hole-in-one insurance for a golf tournament)?

- Are there risks involved with celebrities (hidden expense in the contract, etc.)?

- Will this event have any fallout with donors (a politically incorrect comedian, etc.)?

- Does the event require any seed money your organization cannot afford to front?

- Is there a chance this event could lose money, and if so, can we afford to lose that money?

watch out!

A Word about Collaborative and Third-Party Events

If you do not feel that you have the capability to run a major event, there are several other options. You might want to collaborate with another organization, especially one that has a similar but not directly competing mission. One word of caution is that when embarking on collaborative events, make sure that both organizations are willing to sign an agreement outlining how expenses and income will be shared and how the workload will be divided.

Another option is third-party events, in which another group holds an event and gives the proceeds to your organization. A written agreement should be in place outlining exactly how income and expenses are to be shared. The event organizers should clearly tell the recipient organization how its name, logo, and other information will be used in promoting the event. With the proper written agreement, both third-party and collaborative events can be very successful for organizations that do not have the staff, time, volunteers, or expertise to run an event on their own.

> Special events are just *one* way of raising money for your organization, and might not be the most productive or cost-effective way of raising money. Board members often opt for events because it relieves them of the burden of being involved in directly asking others to support your organization—or because they don't know that there are other, more effective ways to raise money. When it comes to the various types of fundraising and average costs of each method, events rank fairly low on the scale of effectiveness.
>
>
> important

Avoiding Special-Event Overload

Perhaps your organization is already doing multiple events and needs to decide which ones to continue and which ones to drop. Using the above list of questions and the analysis form in **Appendix A** should help you decide which events are the most appropriate for your organization.

On the other hand, if you are bombarded with requests from board and volunteers to add yet another special event to your bag of fundraising tricks, take heed! Many organizations get caught up in "special-event fever" when a board member or other well-meaning volunteer hears about a successful event run by some other organization and decides that your organization should run a similar event.

The first thing you should do is help the board understand that each proposed event has to be closely examined to be sure that the benefits outweigh the costs, *including lost opportunity costs*. Unless you have employees whose job it is to implement special events, when program/ service staff are also asked to manage events, they end up diverting their energies away from their main focus. If you do have development staff, then board members and volunteers need to understand that if the development staff members are busy with events, they might not be able to visit major donors, meet grant deadlines, etc.

The second thing you should do is help the board understand your nonprofit's overall or comprehensive development plan. Make sure that your plan has realistic methods for acquiring sufficient income from diverse sources, including your individual donor strategy, major gift programs, grants strategy, and the like. Once the board sees that you've got it covered, pressure to add special events will likely diminish.

To Recap

◆ We generally recommended that you hold one signature event each year.

◆ Events should, whenever possible, tie into the mission of your organization. For example, a homeless shelter could invite local businesspeople to come in and share breakfast with the shelter guests before asking them to support the shelter financially.

◆ The goals of the events must be clear to all involved. Is it a friend-raiser, a fundraiser, or both? And there should always be a careful analysis done *before* undertaking an event and *after* the event to see if it has met its goals.

◆ Avoid overdependence on special events with a well-thought-out development plan that encompasses all types of fundraising activities. The board members should have input into the development of this plan. If they have bought into the plan, they're less likely to want to deviate from it.

◆ A solid development plan enables many organizations to avoid the temptation to add "just one more" event to their list and focus on more productive ways to raise money.

Chapter Thirteen

Direct Response Fundraising

IN THIS CHAPTER

- ···→ How much can we reasonably expect to raise from a direct-mail appeal?

- ···→ Is telephone fundraising worth the effort?

- ···→ How much time and effort should we spend on direct response fundraising?

To show where you might be going wrong with direct response fundraising, let's review what the Leaky Bucket study tells us about the *results* of marketing and outreach, the practices that bring in the gifts. And these results, believe us, are nothing to write home about.

The Leaky Bucket study shows us that:

- ◆ Only 6 percent of respondents have documented criteria for qualifying their donor prospects, criteria which include wealth profile, giving history, and charitable motivation.

- ◆ Only 13 percent have performance targets that specify how much income the development team is supposed to produce, and from how many donors.

- ◆ And only 9 percent set retention targets that include both income and numbers of retained donors.

This means that more than 41 percent of all respondents lack the basic criteria for prospecting, building relationships, and holding on to donors year after year. If you have not done that basic homework, your direct-response campaigns *will* be less effective. And never forget, a highly successful direct-response campaign will produce responses from only 1 to 3 percent of all recipients. A good response is 1.5 percent; anything above that is considered fantastic.

Let's say you mail out 10,000 letters and your response rate is 1.5 percent. That means that 150 people gave you some kind of response. It also means that 9,850 people put your letter in the trash. Only you can answer the question "was it worth my time and money?" But if you have a good plan in place to renew and upgrade these donors, it might be worth the time and expense even with a low return rate.

Direct mail allows you to reach the most people with the least effort. It is also one of the least productive types of fundraising. However, direct-response fundraising techniques, including mail and email appeals, do have an important role to play in most development programs, as long as you've set realistic and appropriate expectations. And some direct mail should be aimed at "friend-raising" and strengthening the connection with current constituents, not simply asking for money.

There are several types of direct mail that should play an important role in your overall fundraising program:

Think about this: How will our donors feel if the only time they hear from us is when we're asking for money!

- ◆ Acquisition mailings

- ◆ Renewal mailings

- ◆ Cultivation mailings

- ◆ Acknowledgment mailings

What Are Acquisition Mailings and How Are They Used?

Acquisition mailing is the term for direct-response campaigns whose aim is to acquire new donors or donor prospects. It is generally used if you do not already have a built-in base of constituents who could be likely supporters of your fundraising efforts. Some organizations might never use acquisition mailings. A college or university, for example, seldom does acquisition mailings because there is already a donor base of alumni, parents, and friends. Hospitals, likewise, usually have a significant number of "grateful patients" to solicit, so they might not need to conduct acquisition mailings. Religious institutions are also unlikely to use acquisition mailings unless they are attempting to reach out to their community for more members.

On the other hand, if you run a local homeless shelter, domestic violence group, other human service organization, or even a new arts organization, you might use acquisition mailing to counter the fact that you lack an "alumni" base or other natural constituency. Major national disease-related groups often rely heavily on acquisition mailings, based on the premise that they have a universal appeal. Almost everyone has a friend or relative who has had cancer, heart disease, or diabetes. When these groups reach out to the general public for donations, they will be fairly successful because the reader can identify with the cause.

So how do you determine whether an acquisition mailing is right for you? Some questions to ask include:

◆ Do we have a compelling need to acquire new donors?

◆ Can we easily obtain names of individuals who could be potential supporters of our organization?

◆ Can we afford to build the lists we'll need to conduct acquisition mailings?

◆ Do we have the resources and budget to design and produce an attractive mailer that will motivate people to pay attention?

◆ Can we afford the mailings themselves? The budget must include any costs for creating the mailer, producing it, and postage. And we all know what postage costs.

Some ways you can acquire names:

◆ Build your own list

◆ List sharing

◆ List rental

So which is the best option for you?

Building Your Own List

Building your own list is the first strategy to consider. Frankly, we think you must start here, whatever other methods you might use. Ask board members, staff, or volunteers for names of their friends, relatives, or others whom they think may be interested in supporting your organization. This option, however, has limitations because often board members and others are reluctant to pass along names. Even if they do provide names, these friends and relatives might have little interest in your organization's mission.

Some better ways to build your own mailing list include capturing names of people who:

◆ Attend your special events

◆ Visit your website

◆ Subscribe to your electronic newsletter

◆ Download your white papers, videos, or podcasts

◆ Attend your programs

This method is more effective than relying on staff and board members to provide lists because these individuals have already shown an interest in your organization, mission, or programs.

List Sharing

Some organizations will share lists with other organizations that have a similar mission but may not be in direct competition. Of course, if you have no list to share in return, it might be hard to convince even a friendly organization to provide its list. Also, the *Donor Bill of Rights* and some state laws require that if you share your list, you must give donors the opportunity to opt out of having their names given to other organizations. And don't forget that there is federal legislation governing the use of lists for marketing purposes. When creating electronic lists, you can use opt-in methods, whereby you give the contact the option to say no to your invitation to accept mailings.

List Rental

The most effective way to ensure that you can get a mailing list of people who are interested in your mission is to rent lists. A list broker can provide names and addresses of individuals who are likely to be interested in your organization. List brokers will rent names usually for a one-time use or a time-limited use, say one year, meaning that you can mail to these individuals as many times as you want within that specified time period.

The advantage of renting a list from a reputable list broker is that you can identify individuals with an interest in your cause. For example, an environmental group can rent lists of subscribers to outdoor magazines whose readers will likely be interested in protecting the environment. In addition, the names to be rented can be qualified in a number of ways, including household income, age, ethnicity, zip code, or owners of property. Be aware, however, that the more qualifiers put on the list, the more expensive the rental charges will be.

It is also possible to buy lists from list brokers outright and to contract with them for regular updates to these lists. This is a relatively costly strategy, however, so be judicious when using it.

Deciding on Acquisition Mailings

In most cases, direct-mail acquisition costs anywhere from $1.25 to $1.50 for every dollar you raise. However, the long-term benefit of acquisition mailing often outweighs this initial cost because once you receive a gift from a mail donor, this donor becomes yours. Direct mail offers a tremendous opportunity to build a strong relationship with the donor that can result in renewed and increased gifts.

Another advantage of acquisition mailings is the "hanging around" factor. When you mail someone a flyer, invitation, or brochure, you can expect that document to hang around the individual's home or office, thus creating more opportunities for the individual to read and consider it. The one piece of a direct-mail appeal that tends to hang around the longest is the response envelope, so be sure to put some thought and effort into this piece.

The most important thing to remember is that you must have a strategy to renew and upgrade donors acquired through this method. Be aware that the average response rate on acquisition mailings is only 0.5 to 1.5 percent. On the other hand, sending direct mail to individuals who already know and support your organization usually yields a response of 10 to 20 percent.

Many major donors and even planned givers have started their relationships with their preferred charities after first being approached through an acquisition mailing.

food for thought

The Direct-Mail Package

Direct mail is more than just writing a letter. The whole package needs to be considered:

◆ What will the outside (or carrier) envelope look like?

◆ Who will write the letter, who will sign the letter, and how long should it be?

◆ What type of response form will be used?

◆ What other information should be included?

◆ Is your mailing list accurate?

The Outside Envelope

The outside envelope is important because if the package is not inviting, chances are your letter will not even be opened. For small mailings, first-class stamps are the most effective. For large mailings and acquisition mail, nonprofit bulk-rate stamps are often just as effective. A message or a photo on the outside envelope can also be very effective in encouraging individuals to open mail.

If you are going to handle the mailing in-house, meet with the bulk-mail staff of your post office. Consider advantages and disadvantages of bulk mail, first-class mail, and other choices. Also, meet with representatives of mail houses. Often, you can save time and money by working with an established company, typically called a mail house. You might be able to negotiate favorable terms with the mail house for its services, but always remember that a mail house cannot give you a discount on the postage itself.

Never use labels on the outside envelope. A personalized printing that looks like a hand-typed envelope or even a handwritten envelope is much more effective and is easily done if you have the right technology. And if you can get a key community leader to sign the letter, this person might even offer to send the letter on personal or company letterhead and envelopes.

The Letter

Having a high-profile community leader, preferably a board member or other volunteer with the organization, sign the letter is much more effective than sending a letter signed by your CEO or other staff member. A volunteer provides credibility to your organization and lets the reader know that the community supports your organization. Make sure, however, that the letter is professionally written and tells your story. The volunteer can add personal touches to the letter before it is ready for printing.

The length of the letter varies depending on your audience. Many direct-mail experts say a three- or four-page letter is the most effective. Some people, however, will not read more than a one-page letter. Test a few approaches to see what your prospective donors respond to best. A good rule of thumb to follow is that the letter should be as long as it takes to tell your story. The story is drawn from your case for support.

Always use a personalized inside address and greeting. The first paragraph should be a "grabber" that will keep the reader interested in reading more. The letter must contain a call to action or the ask. It is always best to ask for a specific amount of money, to ask higher rather than lower, and to tell donors how their money will be used. A P.S. is often used to reiterate important concepts or to stress the urgency of the appeal.

Enclosures

You might wonder how effective it is to enclose brochures, photos, or token giveaways like labels or bookmarks with your direct-mail piece. We find that most people would rather see their money spent on the programs than on "tchotchkes," but there are many exceptions to this rule. It is important to test your audience and see if giveaways will work with your donors.

The Response Piece

The response piece is the most important part of your direct-mail package. The outside envelope, while important, is usually the first thing to get thrown away, followed by the letter, and then the enclosures. The one piece that individuals generally save the longest is the response envelope. It makes sense, therefore, to spend a lot of thought on what the response envelope and pledge card should look like. A larger response envelope (#9, nine inches) stands out more than a smaller one (#6, six inches) and gives the opportunity for individuals to enclose larger-sized checks (in inches, and sometimes in dollars). Provide options for people to select the amount of their gifts from a list, starting with the highest amounts first.

Your Mailing List

No matter how you obtain your mailing list, accuracy is of primary importance. Nothing turns off a potential donor more than being addressed improperly. A misspelled name, a Mr. and Mrs. salutation to individuals no longer married, or a Mr. addressed to a woman, can make the difference between gaining a gift and having the letter tossed in the trash without even being opened. If your mailing list is internal, be sure it is kept up to date and reviewed before each mailing. If you are obtaining a list from an outside source such as a list broker or another nonprofit, ask for references and talk to these references about the accuracy of the broker's lists.

Make it easy for people to opt out. In the body of the letter, include a website address (URL) or a toll-free phone number that the individual may go to online or call to be removed from your mailing list.

Renewal Mailings

You can also use direct mail to renew and upgrade donors. You need to have a plan for building relationships that leads to renewed and increased gifts.

Renewal mailings should always include the amount of the donor's last gift and a specific request to increase the size of the next gift. Be certain to let donors know that their previous gifts were appreciated and how the money was used to further your mission. Renewal and upgraded gifts through direct mail should be analyzed on an annual basis. When you review the performance of a renewal mailing, ask yourself questions such as these:

◆ How many donors renewed?

◆ How many donors upgraded?

◆ How many donors lapsed (did not renew)?

◆ What was the overall dollar increase in gifts?

◆ What were the costs of renewal mailings?

◆ What was the average gift size, and did it increase or decrease from previous mailings?

◆ What is our strategy at some point in the coming year for phoning or visiting individuals who gave at or above a certain level?

Donor Fatigue

One question that often arises is "How often should we send direct-mail campaigns to the same donor?" The answer is: Test, test, test! One way to do this is to pull out small groups and send one group monthly mailings and mail to another group two or three times a year. Wait for the responses to see which option performed better. Once you've tested different approaches, use the most productive schedule for the remainder of the list.

Another option is to ask your donors, through surveys or focus groups, how often they want to hear from you.

It is important to know if your donors respond better to more frequent or less frequent mailings. But, keep in mind that your budget will dictate how frequently you use direct mail. For many organizations, a once-a-year mail campaign is sufficient, often at year-end (November or early December) when individuals are considering tax consequences of their charitable giving and are often in a more generous mood. Renewal mailings can also be used to encourage monthly giving with an option to contribute using a credit card or through an online payment system such as PayPal.

Cultivation Mailings

You can use direct mail in many ways. Cultivation mailings such as program updates, newsletters, annual reports, and surveys can also be used to build relationships with donors. People who have a relationship with you want to hear from you not just when you're asking for money. They want to know what you are doing, how you are helping the community, and perhaps even how they can become involved as volunteers. So, what are some of the other ways you can communicate with donors through the mail (electronic or "snail mail")?

Newsletters

Your newsletter can be either in hard copy, electronic, or both. Be sure that your newsletter actually contains "news," not the monthly lunch menu in the cafeteria. News can be:

◆ Program updates

◆ Staff and board appointments

◆ Personal success stories from program participants

◆ Personal stories from donors

◆ News about expanded programs and facilities

All these are newsworthy items that can inspire and motivate donors. Most donors love to see their names in print, so list donors unless they have requested anonymity.

Your newsletter should feature your mission and vision statements prominently and list your board of directors. A response envelope should be included with newsletters mailed through the post office for those who want to make donations, and for electronic newsletters, make sure there is a link to an online donations page, a coupon for making a donation, or some other electronic method to promote a reaction from the reader.

Annual Reports

Your annual report does not have to look like the expensive publication General Motors or IBM sends its stockholders. But an interesting and well-written annual report can be a great donor cultivation tool. You are most likely required to submit information annually to the Internal Revenue Service, and this information will be available to donors by searching the Internet. Why not use this opportunity for another communication and send it to donors and prospective donors? Add some photos and some stories about program successes and the organization's plans for the future. Include a list of donors for the year. You can send the annual report to all your donors along with a note from the board chair, post it on your website, or preferably both!

Acknowledgment Mailings

You should always thank donors within twenty-four hours of the time their donation is received. This provides donors with acknowledgment that their checks were indeed received, but it also lets them know that you value their relationship. Handwritten notes on thank-you letters are a good way to show donors that you really care about them and know them personally.

An occasional letter just to let donors know how you are doing and how you are using their contributions to truly make a difference is needed to build the type of relationships that result in long-term commitment and major gifts. Effective use of the mail can play a major role in helping build a successful fundraising campaign.

Telephone Fundraising

Many organizations dread the "T" word, because they think telephone calls are intrusive. However, studies have proven that telephone fundraising is more effective than direct-mail campaigns. Statistics also show that most individuals do not complain to authorities about calls from individuals in their community raising funds for local nonprofits. They *do* complain about the storm window salespeople, the credit card telemarketers, "robo-calls," and other similar calls.

In addition to using the phone to solicit gifts, you can use the phone for a number of other purposes, including:

◆ To invite previous donors to upgrade their gifts

◆ To ask for pledges to a capital campaign

◆ To identify prospects for planned gifts

◆ To survey donors about your case for support

◆ To thank donors for their gifts

Best Prospects for Telephone Fundraising

The first rule of using the phone effectively for fundraising is that you call people who know your organization. They are members, donors, alumni, or users of your services. Never make cold calls to people who do not know your organization or have no affiliation with your mission.

How Many Prospects Do We Need in Our Database for a Phone Campaign?

Phone appeals can be made to a few dozen, several hundred, or tens of thousands of individuals.

Who Should Make the Calls?

The main factor is the number of people on your list to be called. If, for example, you are planning to call a group of a few dozen major donors to thank them for their gifts, you can ask board members to come thirty minutes prior to a board meeting to make these calls.

If you have several hundred members you want to call to renew or upgrade memberships, you can enlist a team of a few dozen volunteers to work at a phonathon. For a phonathon, all the callers are in the same room. They can use a "phone bank" or bring their cell phones and make the calls.

However, if you have thousands of names to be called, we recommend that you engage a professional telephone fundraising firm to handle that volume. Or, when calling for a specialized purpose such as capital campaign or planned giving, a professional firm might be the best option.

Volunteer Phonathons

For a phonathon, you can find volunteers from among:

◆ current users of your services;

◆ previous users of services (alumni);

- ◆ current members or donors;

- ◆ board members;

- ◆ volunteers from local businesses or service clubs.

All volunteers will need to be trained before making calls. Make sure they are totally familiar with your organization and its programs, especially the particular project or program for which they are seeking funding. A list of talking points will be critical. It is best not to have volunteers read directly from a "canned script" but rather to take the talking points and put them into their own words. They will sound more sincere and less like a telemarketer. They might want to write up a "script" for the first few calls until they get into a rhythm and to practice by calling a few good friends or relatives first.

Some tips on handling customary objections will also help them feel more at ease on the phone. Of course, be sure to instruct them not to use any high-pressure techniques to obtain pledges. They also need to be instructed on how to complete the phonathon forms and tally their totals unless you have a volunteer or staff person to handle this aspect of the phonathon.

Make sure your volunteers feel appreciated. Providing token gifts such as a T-shirt or coffee mug can be enough. Many volunteers are motivated by the competition of getting the most pledges, the largest pledge of the evening, or completing the most calls. Some nice items such as gift certificates to popular local restaurants can inspire volunteers and add to the fun of the phonathon.

Using Professional Callers

If you have more than a thousand names to be called or the ask is for a specialized project like planned giving or a capital campaign, it is usually best to hire a professional telephone fundraising firm to do the calling. Look for a professional telephone fundraising firm that works exclusively with nonprofits and will work on a flat-fee basis. The fee may be based on the number of calls completed or a flat hourly fee. Percentage-based fundraising is unethical.

What Makes a Phone Campaign Successful?

Whether you are using professional callers or volunteers, there are some key aspects of a successful phone campaign.

The List

As with a direct-mail appeal, having an accurate list is a critical part of success. Be sure you have correct names and phone numbers. People today tend to be very mobile. They get married and divorced, change their phone numbers, and even eliminate landlines and use cell phones exclusively. If you feel your list is not accurate, spend some time "cleaning it up." You can contract this task out to a firm designed to do this in order to make sure addresses and phone numbers are accurate. This can save you a lot of time, money, and frustration.

The Precall Letter

Always plan to send a letter out before calls are made. This gives legitimacy to the call and can lay the groundwork for a successful call. Finding the right letter signer is an important part of the process. Letters should be signed by a volunteer, preferably one with a high community profile and one who will be warmly received by the individual receiving the letter.

Do not tell readers to send a donation "so they won't be called." This gives the donor the idea that the phone call is punishment for not sending in a donation. The letter should state that this is an important project so you want to talk to the donor personally about it. As with stand-alone direct mail, the letter and any supporting material should be based on the case for support.

The Calls

When you are using volunteers to make the calls, they should begin every call by saying that they are volunteers for your organization. They should next ask if the prospective donor has received the precall letter and ask if the donor has any questions. The caller should then ask the prospective donor about any past or current involvement with your organization. If the prospect is a past donor, the caller should express the organization's gratitude for past support.

Both professional callers and volunteers should always ask for a specific pledge amount, based on the donor's previous history with your organization and the caller's sense of the phone call. A phone appeal can be a very effective way to encourage a donor to upgrade to a higher level. For an initial gift, ask for the largest amount the donor is expected to give. For example, if you believe the donor will give from ten to fifty dollars, ask for a fifty-dollar pledge. For a donor who has given in the past, ask for an amount larger than the amount of the most recent gift. With larger donations, do not increase the ask amount too much; a 10 or 20 percent increase is usually appropriate. With smaller donors, you might want to ask for an amount double the previous gift—for example, asking a twenty-five-dollar donor for fifty dollars this year. If you are using a professional firm, the firm's representative will guide you through the process of setting ask amounts. If using volunteers, a fundraising consultant might help with the letter, the process of setting the amount to request, and the volunteer training.

The Follow-Up

Even though volunteers are well trained, your prospective donors might have questions the callers cannot answer. If this is the case, be sure a process is in place to get back to the donor with the information requested. Some donors might prefer not to be called. If a donor requests to be removed from future phonathon lists, be sure to honor this request and to make note of this preference on the database so this donor is not called in the future. Be sure that the callers thank donors for their past support. Callers should always graciously thank the people they have called for their time, whether or not they have made a pledge. It is important to lay the groundwork for a future ask. Remember, a "no" is not always "no forever."

Collecting pledges after a phonathon is obviously an important step. One practice that helps collection rates tremendously is sending out the pledge forms the very next day. Include a return envelope so individuals can easily write a check and drop it in the mail. All the forms should be prepared the night of the phonathon. If a professional firm is being used, the company will handle this. For a volunteer phonathon, you might have some volunteers who do not like to make phone calls, and you can ask these volunteers to help with tallying results and preparing the pledge confirmations for mailing.

To Recap

◆ Direct mail, while not the most effective or efficient way to raise money, is an important part of your overall development plan. Many major donors and even planned-giving donors started out by making gifts of fifty, twenty-five, or even ten dollars through a mail appeal.

◆ Direct mail and phone appeals are important because they allow you to build relationships with your donors—relationships that will help move them up the donor pyramid.

◆ Using information from your mail and phone programs to build your overall development program is critical. First, be sure to record any address or name changes, those who wish to be removed from future phone or mail lists, donors who want to remain anonymous, or any other pertinent information gained during the calling process. Review the performance of every campaign religiously; you need to know what worked, what didn't, what ought to be changed, and what needs to stay.

◆ Making contacts by phone will often elicit valuable insights that can help in future solicitations with donors, such as their interest in a particular program. All this information needs to be entered into your donor database along with the amount of the pledge.

◆ Remember, mail and phone campaigns should occasionally be used for things other than raising money. Use your direct-response program to inform donors of your activities and to let them know they're appreciated and how their money was used. This will go a long way toward building long-term relationships and increased giving levels form your donors.

Chapter Fourteen

In-Person Solicitation

IN THIS CHAPTER

- ···→ Why you need to profile your ideal donor

- ···→ Understanding the exchange of value between donor and charity

- ···→ Three simple questions that create donor trust

- ···→ Bigger pie, bigger slice: in-person solicitation as a driver for well-balanced fund diversification

In-person solicitation is the most common and effective strategy for implementing great major-gift programs and robust corporate relations. The size of the gifts and the prospect of long-term relationships that you seek in these funding categories justify a hefty investment of time, effort, and money on your part.

There are four ways you can go wrong in your in-person solicitation strategies. And if you don't know what can go wrong, you've got one foot on a banana peel.

The first way to go wrong is to fail to have a well-thought-out, documented ideal-funder profile. Yet the Leaky Bucket study tells us that only 6 percent of respondents have a documented ideal-donor profile that includes donor motivation and preferences as well as the standard wealth profile. Even worse is to have such a profile but fail to use it rigorously. If you or your development people say that choosing the right prospects is an "art," that they have great "intuition," and that they "don't need no stinkin' profiles," we suggest you talk to them gently but firmly.

The second way is to ask for a gift too soon in the cultivation process. This phenomenon often occurs with inexperienced people or volunteer solicitors who may be anxious about the whole asking-for-money thing. But asking for gifts before building a relationship is all too common. It's an easy way to blow it with the prospect.

The third way is to lack metrics that help you figure out the next steps you'll need to take in order to move your prospect toward a desired end result. Once you have the right metrics or milestones of the process in place, you and your development team always know what to do next.

Fourth, neither you nor your volunteer solicitors have mastered the art of the probing question, a special questioning technique that (a) rules out the DOAs, (b) helps you figure out how much effort to invest in prospects, and (c) gets prospects to tell you how to cultivate them *and* close the deal. Without those insights, you may fail to build relationships at all, or you may confuse the prospects.

Ha. Bet you expected us to talk about how to make the ask! Actually, that's the least problematic issue of all, as you'll see. From where we stand, getting the process right in the first place is what makes the difference.

The Tragedy of Nonprofit Nonqualifying: What the Leaky Bucket Study Tells Us

Qualifying a prospect is pretty much like finding out if the prospect is good enough for you, not the other way around. Good qualifying techniques help development professionals avoid the "tin cup" mentality: "Gee whiz, we need money!!! Will you give me some?" Instead, you take the high road by saying to yourself, "Hmm, let me see if it's worth my time to cultivate you."

About the worst thing you can do is ignore the need for a well-defined and carefully documented

> The term "qualifying" describes the process of gathering information about a prospect in order for you to decide that the prospect has the right wealth profile (net worth, giving history), and charitable philosophy (already gives to similar causes, etc.) to justify further cultivation.

Definition

profile for each major funding category. We discussed the need for this profile in **Chapters One**, **Two**, and even **Chapter Three** on metrics. The ideal-funder profile is a type of benchmark. You use this benchmark to qualify the prospect to see how close the prospect comes to resembling the benchmark. A prospect that's a good match is far more likely to give to you; one that's a poor match is less likely to give to you.

It takes a long time to cultivate a new major donor. Don't waste even more time trying to win over a donor that doesn't fit your criteria.

◆ Without a documented profile, anybody in the organization can pursue any prospect. The selection criteria are missing.

◆ Without the guidance of a profile, you or your team can chew up a lot of hours trying to cultivate a mediocre prospect (or a DOA).

We learned that 6 percent of all Leaky Bucket study respondents said they have absolutely no ideal-funder profile for any category. And 61 percent said they had only "preferences" but no documented profiles. This tells us that 67 percent of nonprofits studied have no method to guide their development officers to invest their time in high-potential donors and avoid wasting it on low-potential prospects.

leaky bucket results

◆ Without a benchmark that you've all agreed to accept, prospect selection is subjective. If there's a dispute about the prospect's potential, there's no way to assess the potential. It all comes down to which development officer or volunteer can shout the loudest.

◆ Can you or your team distinguish between a prospect who's warm and gracious but lacks the wealth or motivation to give and one who *also* has the right level of wealth and passion for your cause? You just don't get the gifts without both characteristics.

On the other hand, when organizations have and use their ideal-funder profiles, they discover that it actually takes *more* time to cultivate a prospect that's a "C" or "D" than it does to cultivate a prospect that's an "A," and the size of the gifts is larger from the As.

Building Your Profile: Three Categories

Donor-prospect research is always a hot topic in fundraising circles, as well it should be. To build your organization's ideal-donor profile, you need to know what should go into this research. To perform effective donor research, you need to list the selection criteria first. That's why we call it the "ideal" donor profile; you're going to design the perfect funder for yourself first and then go out and see who looks like a match.

The Fact Profile

The fact profile is that portion of your ideal-donor profile that describes hard criteria such as age, gender, level of education, and so on, information that is usually available in the public record. Once you've decided what those criteria should be, go out and look for prospects who share those characteristics. There are many database services and other resources that can be used to find hundreds or even thousands of candidates who match these criteria. They include some familiar names such as WealthEngine.com, LexisNexis, the Foundation Directory (if you are seeking grants), and many others. Some of them require costly subscriptions, while others may be found at your public library or the library of a university.

The LAI Principle

To get a major gift, you must have identified the following in your prospective donors:

Linkage: Do you have someone who can open the door to this prospect?

Ability: Does the prospect have the ability to make a major gift?

Interest: Is the prospect interested in your organization and/or the types of programs you offer?

food for thought

Before you start paying subscription fees, look at your current base of donors, even if it's still small. Concentrate on the donors who have given you the largest gifts, have given to you regularly over several years, or have given you progressively larger gifts over the years. Ask yourself what characteristics they have in common. Is it age, gender, zip code, educational background, giving history?

Documenting the fact profile is an excellent start, but so far, you've created only about a third of the donor profile.

The Qualitative Characteristics

Once you know your ideal prospect's wealth profile and giving history, you're not done. You still don't know about the prospect's motivations for giving or charitable philosophy. If you don't know *why* the prospect gives, you won't know what it takes to attract this prospect and motivate a gift to your organization.

Go back to that list of past and current donors again. Now think about the ones you like the most. What is it you like about them? Again, look for the qualities or values or characteristics that occur most often in your list of "favorite" donors. Ignore their wealth and even the size of their gifts. Here are some fairly typical qualitative characteristics that you might like to include (we're sure you can think of others):

◆ They have a real passion for your mission or cause or programs.

◆ They have a real concern about the issues your mission addresses. In other words, they are worried about what might happen if nonprofits like yours can't do the job.

◆ They have experience with the issue or mission. In other words, they were a client and you really helped them, they needed the services you provide but couldn't find them, or you helped a friend or relative, and they're grateful to you.

Some people may be motivated to give to charity for reasons that might seem self-serving to you. Perhaps they want to be known widely for their philanthropy. Yes, every donor, no matter how small the gift, wants and deserves some recognition from you, but not everybody wants their names in lights (or on your building). Maybe the donor wants to be associated with other major donors who represent a social circle to which this donor aspires. Maybe the donor thinks that being recognized as a donor to your organization will offer social prestige. Don't ignore such motivations even if you believe them to be "politically incorrect."

As you identify these characteristics, you should also ask yourself "What would I need to say in order to show the prospect that what we do is a good match to this donor's reasons for giving?"

The "Danger Signs"

Sometimes you will find a prospect with the right fact profile who also seems to embody the right qualitative characteristics, but this person is hard to deal with. How hard should you work to bring in a gift from this donor? Consider the danger signs, those indicators that this prospect will cost too much to win over or, if you do win the donor over, that you'll end up sorry because your life is miserable. Pay attention to these danger signs! Nothing's worse than spending thousands of hours to land a major donor who likes to "stir the pot" or demands more attention and recognition than the gift warrants.

Think through the tip-offs that could signal that you're in danger. Here are a few:

◆ The prospect "turns off" when talk turns to money.

◆ You can't actually get close to the prospect; everything has to go through layers of attorneys and financial advisors.

◆ You have reason to believe that the donor's family members are battling over the donor's wealth and you're ending up in the middle.

◆ After a great warm start, suddenly the donor won't return your phone calls.

Building Your Profile

Once you've selected the criteria for each category, write up your document. We like to set up a spreadsheet where we can list all the criteria in one column. Then in the second column, we state whether the criterion is of high importance, moderate importance, or low importance. The third column allows you to show how well the prospect matches the particular criterion; again, this donor is a high match, moderate match, or low match to each criterion. (For the danger signs, you always want low match! You *don't* want your prospects to embody such criteria.) Once you have completed every criterion, decide whether on balance the prospect offers you high, moderate, or low potential.

Now you know whom to pursue or invest in.

Three Simple Questions That Establish Donor Trust

The way to conduct effective in-person solicitation is by cultivating your ability to ask questions.

Yes, you heard us right. Where conventional wisdom always reminds us to be a good listener, we say there's not much point in listening to any old random dialog. What you want to do is to hear the right *answers*, answers that tell you (a) how well the prospect matches your ideal-donor profile and (b) if there is a match, what the donor wants to see or hear from you that indicates yours is the right charity to invest in.

To get the right answers, you have to know how to ask the right questions. The right questions provoke a dialog between donor and fundraiser that establishes trust and rapport, giving prospects permission to speak at length about themselves and their careers, charitable motivations, philosophies, and expectations. With such insights, you and your fundraising team can listen for the answers that tell whether the donor justifies the investment of your time and attention. The right questions help prospects tell you how—and whether—to cultivate them.

> What should you do with prospects who offer low potential? By all means, accept their gifts, but don't spend a lot of time on them. Time is money. Remember, your fundraising time is probably worth $1,000 per hour or more. It doesn't make sense for you to spend even an hour to cultivate a twenty-five-dollar gift using in-person solicitation. Instead, influence these low-potential donors through a combination of mass-marketing techniques such as direct mail, direct email, online donations, and special events. The cost per gift is amortized across the entire campaign or event.
>
> **watch out!**

Here are the Three Simple Questions:

1. The Success Question: "What do you want to achieve?"

2. The Frustration Question: "What do you want to avoid?"

3. The "Right-Charity" Question: "What helps you decide which charity to support?"

> There might be a very good reason that human beings are born with *one* mouth and *two* ears!
>
> **food for thought**

These questions work because they put the development officer and the prospect at the level of peers. Experienced donors have seen every fundraising trick in the book. They are immune to self-serving language, forcing, or other coercive techniques. They can sniff out a fundraiser who lacks confidence in a heartbeat. Inexperienced donors may be intimidated by some techniques, even alienated by fundraisers who feel awkward. Peer solicitors, who typically are not fundraising professionals, might experience "ask reluctance," fear of engaging with prospective donors, and end up asking the wrong questions at the wrong time. Or just refuse to solicit at all.

You will want to make sure that volunteers are trained in how to ask the right questions and listen for the right answers. These questions, and their many variations, change the conversation to one of respectful interest centered on the donor and the donor's reasons for giving, personal advancement, reputation building, desire to redress wrongs, or any other sentiment that provokes charitable giving. Questions such as these create an atmosphere that gives both parties permission to say "We are not really right for one another" and still part on good terms. And that answer is a desirable one, indeed, considering the cost of your scarce and precious time, if you want to invest in prospects with good potential for high lifetime value.

The Success Questions: "What Do You Want to Achieve?"

Always start with success questions. Ask your prospect "What do you want to achieve with your charitable donations?" There are many different ways to ask this question, and you can ask it many different times in the course of your relationship. You're basically asking the prospect to answer the question "What's in it for you?" Some variations include:

> Read John Greenhoe's excellent book *Mastering the Discovery Call: Opening the Door to Major Gifts*, for more on the fine art of questioning—and listening—to cultivate major-donor prospects.
>
> **food for thought**

◆ Why is supporting Cause X important to you?

◆ When you think about other charities you have supported in the past, what was most important to you?

◆ What led you to support Charity X or Agency Y?

◆ When you think about your experience with our charity, what do you like the most about it?

Notice that the prospect cannot answer "yes" or "no" to any of these questions. And that's a good thing, especially early in the game. These are open-ended questions, which means there is no simple answer. By contrast, questions that provoke "yes" or "no" answers are described as "closed," or "close-ended," questions. They may shut down two-way conversations.

The Frustration Question: What Do You Want to Avoid?

This is an interesting question, one which we don't think is asked often enough. The success question drives the prospect to think about what he or she wants to accomplish. But the "avoid" question asks the prospect to explore the conditions or situations that your nonprofit is designed to alleviate. This question asks the prospect "What social, economic, or personal considerations trouble you enough that you'd donate money to alleviate them?"

> An example of a success question, designed for a hospice program:
>
> Question: "When you think about hospice programs such as ours, what motivates you to support them?"
>
> Answer that you'd like to hear: "I really want to see your standard of care provided to everyone nearing the end of life. It's a beautiful thing, what you're doing here."
>
> **Example**

The frustration question is the flip side, or psychological opposite, of the success question. As you become more skillful at using the frustration question and its variations, you'll discover that the prospect gives you answers that complement the success question. They give you invaluable material for your marketing messages.

The Right-Charity Question: "What Helps You Decide Which Charity to Support?"

The right-charity question is a little more subtle than the first two questions. This one elicits some insights into your prospect's criteria for choosing among the many nonprofits that could be beneficiaries of their philanthropy. It's worth the effort to master, since you get such valuable feedback from it, without running the risk of embarrassing the prospect.

After all, it's very likely that your prospects will already be making charitable donations to other nonprofits, missions, causes, and even programs. By attempting to cultivate gifts for your charity, you're asking them to either add you to your list of charities or replace a charity they currently support with gifts to your agency. So you'll want to know how they go about choosing their philanthropic "targets," so to speak, and then deciding that (a) you'll never be able to live up to their expectations, so you should part on good terms, (b) you can become part of their charitable portfolio, and perhaps grow from a relatively minor player to a higher level over time, or (c) you could be one of their major charities.

> **Frustration Question for the Same Hospice Program**
>
> Question: "If hospice programs such as ours were not readily available in our area, what would bother you about that?"
>
> Answer: "You know, when my Aunt Tallulah was suffering so, my cousins and I just couldn't stand it; we simply couldn't provide the kind of care she needed. I refuse to see any other old person like Auntie T have to go through what she went through."
>
> **Example**

It's important to frame the right-charity questions with care. You *don't* want to ask, "How come you support Charity X and not us?" Nor do you want to ask, "What would it take for you to stop supporting Charity X and support us instead?" These heavy-handed approaches might generate a punch in the nose.

Ask the Right Probing Questions, and You Won't Have to "Make the Ask"

We've always believed that conventional training for solicitation places far too much emphasis on what you should do and say, or not do and say, in order to get the prospect to give you a gift. However, we think that if you've cultivated the relationship effectively, then the ask makes itself, so to speak. You reach a point where both of you realize that you're now discussing how *much* money the prospect's ready to give, for which purpose or program, and how to provide the appropriate level of recognition.

Learn instead how to emphasize, opening the opportunity and cultivating the relationship. You'll do that by using these open-ended questions that give prospects permission to talk (often at length) about themselves. Everybody *loves* to talk about themselves, but they don't often get the opportunity, and it's usually considered bad form to do so—except in this context. In this context, you're giving the prospect permission. In fact, you're showing that you're downright eager to know all about the prospect's hopes, dreams, and aspirations.

Another paradoxical thing happens when you master these questioning techniques. Somehow, some way, you—the questioner—become an expert in the eyes of the prospect, even if you frankly don't know all that much about the individual, the prospect's business background, or anything else about this prospect. By placing your focus on the

---

Useful Examples of the Right-Charity Question

◆ How do you choose the charities you want to support? What would you have to see or hear from a nonprofit in order for you to make a significant commitment?

◆ What would a charity need to show you, after you've made your gift, to convince you that you had made a wise investment?

◆ When selecting a charity, what is uppermost in your mind?

◆ Have you ever decided not to invest in a charity or even withdrawn your support from one? Why did that happen?

◆ When you think about other charities that you have supported or currently support, what did you like best about them? Why was that important to you?

◆ What about charities that disappointed you or that you would be reluctant to invest in, other than their mission or cause? Why did they disappoint you, what were you trying to avoid?

Example

prospect's interests, hopes, and dreams, you will come across as a highly sympathetic listener who is genuinely interested in the other person.

And you won't even be faking it.

But What Should I Tell the Prospect?

The process of solicitation is a two-way street. Is this prospect right for you? Are you right for the prospect? Learn to listen "between the lines" so to speak, so you can tell enough about your nonprofit to make the prospect feel comfortable with you, just as you're trying to figure out if you can live with the prospect.

But don't do a long-winded "data dump." Listen for clues.

The answers you'll hear when you ask the right-charity questions give you wonderful reasons to describe what you do, how you do it, how well it works, why other donors love you, and what this donor prospect should expect if the prospect decides to make a major gift.

Even better, you'll find out if you are able to meet donor expectations. If you are, you'll simply say you can and give an example or two. If you can't, you can say something like "We usually don't do it like that; our approach is more like this. Would that work for you?" If you're sure, based on what you've heard, that you really are not the right agency for the prospect, you get to say something like "Oh, I'm so sorry, but we're not able to [do this, sign that, live up to such a standard, etc., etc.]. I wish we could! May I keep you on our mailing list?"

The Value and Delight of Dropping Prospects Who Don't Make the Grade

Sometimes, the prospect is a dead end, a black hole, a DOA. So, now what do you do? You stop cultivating the opportunity.

This may require more discipline than you think. After all, once you've established rapport, it usually feels pretty good, and you may want to continue "cultivating" the opportunity. But how long can you buy lunch, or football tickets, for a prospect who doesn't match your ideal-donor profile, hasn't made any noises about wanting to support you, or has demonstrated some of the danger signs that should tip you off?

Question: "When you think about hospice programs such as ours, what motivates you to support them?"

Answer that you'd like to hear: "I really want to see your standard of care provided to everyone nearing the end of life. It's a beautiful thing, what you're doing here."

Your response: "Yes, we feel the same. We're so proud of our work. Are you aware that *Daily Planet* has described our program as the gold standard for hospice programs in the Greater Metropolitan area? If you'd like to speak to our medical director about our philosophy of care, I'd be happy to arrange it."

Rationale: you provide a third-party endorsement and direct access to a senior member of the clinical staff.

Question: "If hospice programs such as ours were not readily available in our area, what would bother you about that?"

Answer: "You know, when my Aunt Tallulah was suffering so, my cousins and I just couldn't stand it; we simply couldn't provide the kind of care she needed. I refuse to see any other old person like Auntie T have to go through what she went through."

Your response: "I should have you speak to Mrs. Smith. When she was younger, her mother died at home, and there was nobody to care for her except Mrs. Smith herself. She had to quit her job, and it took such a toll on her and her kids. When her husband's father had a stroke last year, she didn't even think about trying to take care of him; she called us immediately."

Rationale: You demonstrated empathy and gave a reference to a client.

food for thought

Guess what? If the prospect's not right for you, you're probably not right for the prospect either. You don't have to tell the prospect "Yuck, we hate you, go away, take your wallet with you, and never darken our door again!" In fact, you don't have to tell the prospect much of anything. You simply stop reaching out. If you were calling every week, drop back to every two weeks, once a month, and less frequently. Keep the prospect's name on your subscription list, include the prospect in the annual appeal, send invitations to your golf tournament or gala. But don't continue to pour your expensive, irreplaceable time into a prospect that offers you low potential for long-term value.

To Recap

◆ Understand how and why some prospects justify your time and effort and some don't.

◆ Document the criteria you use to assess prospect potential; don't just wing it.

◆ Recognize the three key ingredients of a major gift: linkage, ability, and interest.

◆ Master your ability to ask the right questions so you can listen for the right answers.

◆ Hone your ability to listen, "hear" between the lines, and respond appropriately.

Chapter Fifteen

Corporate Fundraising

IN THIS CHAPTER

--→ How much money can we reasonably expect to raise from the local business community?

--→ How do we get to the decision makers?

--→ What are some of the pockets of corporate philanthropy we can tap into?

Corporate contributions account for only about 5 percent of all the philanthropic giving in the United States. When you analyzed your current level of funding diversification (in **Chapter Ten**), what percentage of total income stems from corporate relationships? How much could you raise if you break through the "steel and glass" ceiling of corporate America?

The Leaky Bucket study results for fund diversification were slightly better than we had anticipated, with the largest portion of respondents (49 percent) stating that their income came from a variety of sources but that diversification was not well balanced. That's relatively good. Although the study doesn't tell us the proportion of funding from corporations, there's plenty of room for improvement. And we think that nonprofits as a whole are missing out on a very meaningful stream of income.

So how do we improve that low percentage of money coming from the business community? Well, let's look at the facts first.

Some facts that skew the traditional corporate giving statistics:

◆ Most reports on corporate giving focus on corporate *philanthropic* budgets and don't include corporate sponsorships and other money that comes from the marketing departments of companies.

◆ Matching gifts are typically counted as individual giving.

◆ Giving from corporate foundations often gets counted as foundation giving or grants income.

◆ Building relationships with corporate leaders often leads to personal gifts from those leaders—more individual giving.

observation

So now that we understand some facts, let's look at the various pockets of corporate philanthropy that you might tap into.

Types of Corporate Support

First of all, remember that commercial businesses that give to nonprofit organizations are motivated by something that isn't as common among individual donors, and that is because there is something in it for the business. In other words, the top executives at the business agree that they will gain additional customers, recognition for good corporate citizenship, or something else that has explicit value to their business as a result of supporting nonprofit organizations. There are many ways for them to do so. In our society, such ulterior motives for corporate giving should be honored rather than deplored.

There are many ways you can approach your local, and even national, business communities to support your nonprofit. Tapping into one pocket does not mean the other options are closed to you. Often you can ask for support from a combination of these pockets:

◆ Corporate foundation grants

◆ Employee giving through workplace giving programs and/or employee contributions committees

◆ Local branch allocations (i.e., the local retail outlet of a national chain or a local bank branch manager's discretionary fund)

◆ Gifts obtained by the CEO or board members of a corporation

◆ Matching gifts

◆ Gifts-in-kind

◆ Event attendance and/or sponsorship

◆ Program sponsorship or underwriting

◆ Employee volunteer programs

What's wrong with your corporate funding could be that you are not aware of all these types of support or have not developed the right approaches to access all of these types of funding.

In Linda's book *Raise More Money from Your Business Community*, she describes detailed methods to tap into each of these types of funding support. For now, let's concentrate on identifying the companies in your community you can focus on and how to identify, cultivate, and solicit the leaders of these companies.

Identifying Business Prospects for Your Organization

Let's get rid of that "Willie Sutton" mentality that leads many organizations astray. Linda explains that often we target the banks and big companies in our community because "that's where the money is." However, these major companies are also being hit up by dozens, hundreds, or thousands of other nonprofits, depending on the size of your community. So let's look beyond these usual suspects and seek out businesses more closely aligned to our mission and vision.

As we described in **Chapters Thirteen** and **Fourteen** on direct-response fundraising and in-person solicitation, you need to describe the ideal corporate funder for your organization. Which companies have a natural interest in your work, which ones have supported other similar organizations, with which ones do you have a linkage? Remember the LAI principle we talked about in **Chapter Fourteen**? It holds true for businesses and corporations just as it does for individuals. So, let's try to determine which businesses in your community you should be targeting.

One additional factor is critical in assessing potential corporate funders. That's the WIIFM ("What's in it for me?") factor. For commercial businesses, perhaps this should be the WIIFU factor, or "What's in it for us?" Commercial businesses are quite straightforward in considering the potential business benefits they may accrue by donating corporate money to nonprofits or by underwriting nonprofit programs or services through sponsorship.

Commercial business executives are becoming more and more attuned to the benefits of investing in local or national nonprofit causes as a way to further their corporate objectives or make their corporate brands more trustworthy.

As you can see, building relationships with the business community starts with the identification process. Have your board, staff, and volunteers been invited to identify companies with whom they are connected in some way? If not, start by doing some brainstorming with each of these groups to help identify the companies that match your ideal-funder profile.

Cultivating Business Leaders

Once you've identified these companies, chances are there is not much of a connection between the companies and your organization. Let's fix that now.

Plan a series of cultivation events and activities to help business leaders learn more about your organization.

It is important to note that during cultivation activities and events, you are *not* asking these leaders for money; you are simply trying to build relationships. You can ask them the same types of questions you would ask individual donors "What types of organizations do you support and why? What are your company's goals? Do you see a match between your company's goals and our mission? What other companies do you know that would have an interest in what we're doing? How can we better market our organization to businesses? What do you think we can do to make our case stronger?"

Which Companies Meet Your Ideal-Funder Profile?

◆ Where do your clients and staff do business?

◆ What companies in your community align with your mission?

◆ Which local business leaders do your board members know?

◆ Do you serve anyone that represents or is connected with the local businesses?

◆ Have you networked with local business leaders? Which ones?

◆ Do your board members own or manage businesses? Which ones?

◆ Have local business leaders toured your office or attended your events? Which ones?

◆ Are any of your staff members connected to local businesses, i.e., a spouse who holds a leadership position within a company? Which ones?

◆ Does the business utilize corporate donations or sponsorships as part of their marketing strategy, or will you have to educate it?

◆ Would corporate sponsorships improve its relationships with customers or attract new customers?

◆ Does the business look for opportunities for its executives to serve on nonprofit boards?

◆ Does the business have a track record of marketing via nonprofit sponsorships, donations, or volunteer services?

practical
tip

Learning to Speak "Business Speak"

You also need to think more like a businessperson if you want to build relationships with the business community. A few helpful hints in this area:

◆ Keep meetings brief and to the point.

◆ Don't use nonprofit jargon. (Avoid terms like catchment areas and capacity building, or acronyms specific to your agency's area of expertise.)

◆ Show the bottom-line impact of your organization's programs. Using an economic impact statement will mean more to a business leader than a touchy-feely type plea for money.

◆ Ask explicit questions: "What would motivate you or your business to invest in a nonprofit organization? Why would that be important or valuable to you? What experience have you had in supporting nonprofits in the past?"

◆ Operate on "business time," not on "nonprofit time." Business executives tend to make decisions far more quickly, and then act

---

Cultivation Activities and Events for Business Leaders

◆ Invite business leaders to an open house in your organization.

◆ Meet with a different business leader each week for breakfast to ask for advice about your organization's plans and programs.

◆ Ask board members or other volunteers to host a series of business leaders' breakfasts, again asking for advice.

◆ Ask business leaders to serve on a business advisory council.

◆ Ask business leaders for testimonials or other endorsements that you can use in your marketing materials.

◆ Recruit business leaders to serve on your board.

practical tip

on those decisions immediately, than you may be accustomed to in the nonprofit world.

◆ Plan meetings that are compatible with business leaders' schedules. Many business leaders prefer early-morning meetings. Make sure you ask business executives to name their preferences for meeting times.

You also need to be where the business leaders are. You will not find them at meetings of nonprofit executive directors. You will find them at chamber of commerce meetings, economic development councils, manufacturers' association meetings, and professional clubs such as Rotary, Kiwanis, and Lions Clubs. Get out, join, *and attend meetings* of these groups.

Once you've identified and cultivated business leaders enough to build comfortable relationships, then you can start asking more probing questions about how they would like to get involved within your organization. Questions such as:

> Ask for money, and you'll get advice. Ask for advice, and you'll get money.
>
>  practical tip

◆ What types of support does your company provide to community organizations like ours?

◆ Who are the decision makers in your company?

◆ Do you have an employee volunteer program?

◆ How do you measure your company's success, other than financially?

◆ What is the typical amount of a grant or sponsorship your company might make to fund a program such as ours?

◆ Is our program one with which you could see your company getting involved?

◆ When and how should we approach your company for funding?

◆ Could you see yourself volunteering for our organization or serving on our board?

- ◆ How would it benefit your strategic objectives if you became recognized as a sponsor of an organization like ours?

- ◆ How much experience do you have with nonprofit support or using nonprofit involvement as a portion of your marketing strategy?

Note, we still have not asked for money!

Of course, eventually you do have to ask for money, but only after you've answered the questions we've raised here and built a strong enough relationship to know how much to ask for, when to ask, whom to ask, and for what programs to ask.

Who Does the Ask?

Nobody, because businesspeople do not use such language. Businesspeople simply do not "make the ask," nor are they recipients of "the ask." They pitch the project or idea. They consider the opportunity. They make the sale. They close the deal. They win the project or contract. So if you're cultivating a donation, sponsorship, or underwriting from a commercial business, speak in terms that businesspeople use.

Now we can talk about who is going to manage the relationship and close the deal. (We'd call it a sale if we thought you wouldn't yell at us.) In simple terms, the individual who closes the deal and makes the "sale" is the one who manages the relationship. And this depends largely on the nature of the "sale" to be made.

It depends on who has the strongest relationship with the decision maker(s) at the company. If the company's philanthropy is done through a corporate foundation, it will likely be a staff person who prepares a grant request. If the company is a small business in which the company owner makes all the decisions, then it could be a board member, your CEO, or a peer business leader who cultivates the opportunity. Often a peer-to-peer solicitation from another businessperson is the best way to develop a relationship with a business leader. The important thing to remember is that building the relationship first is just as critical in corporate fundraising as it is in individual fundraising.

A Note about Sponsorships

Corporate sponsorships tend to be treated by the commercial business as an investment in marketing, rather than a charitable contribution, no matter how the finances are managed from a tax perspective. Corporate sponsorships provide opportunities for the business to gain recognition from its association with your program, event, or service. For example, a nonprofit that regularly provides an annual gala might cultivate a commercial business to be recognized as the title sponsor of its gala. To that end, the commercial business may purchase billboard advertising as well as ads in the local paper, TV, and radio. The company knows that it is "buying" so-called views or impressions (i.e., opportunities for buyers and consumers to see its brand associated with the nonprofit event), for some sum of money per impression. It's worth it to the company to gain this exposure, especially when the nonprofit has some intimate and beneficial association with the company's brand, services, corporate values, or some other intangibles.

To Recap

◆ There are many ways you can involve your local business community with your organization. But first, you must identify the businesses that meet your ideal funder profile.

◆ Build relationships with business leaders that match your profile, before presenting the opportunity or closing the deal (i.e., making the ask). There are a variety of ways you can accomplish this through cultivation activities and events.

◆ Involve your board and other volunteers. These groups will have connections that a staff member alone will not be able to develop quickly.

◆ Learn to think like a businessperson. Adjust your time schedule and pace, as well as your way of speaking about your program, to meet the needs of the local business community. Get out into the business world and relate with business leaders.

◆ Choose the right team or person to present the opportunity, and don't forget about all the various pockets of corporate philanthropy you can tap into.

Chapter Sixteen

Ethics, Stewardship, and the Law

IN THIS CHAPTER

···→ How do we retain donors and ensure that we are keeping them happy?

···→ What do we need to know about the laws that affect fundraising?

···→ Do ethics really matter?

As we prepare to conclude this book, we want to discuss a couple of areas that are the foundation of any good fundraising program. So why didn't we cover these in the first chapter? We could have, but we wanted you to think about all of the things we've discussed in this book in light of these areas. If the Leaky Bucket study tells us anything, it's "Don't leave the important things to chance. Fix them before they break." This sentiment applies strongly to the areas of ethics, stewardship, and the law. Ask yourself these questions as you develop your plan:

◆ Do we have a plan in place to ensure we acknowledge and recognize donors properly?

◆ Are we using our donors' money the way they intended it to be used?

◆ Are we reporting gifts properly?

◆ Are we following all the laws that govern our fundraising activities?

◆ Do we uphold accepted ethical standards?

Stewardship

Donor stewardship is important! There are more than a million nonprofit organizations in the United States raising funds from individuals, businesses, government agencies, and foundations. You are competing against all of these organizations, and if you are not treating your donors right, they will find an organization that does!

Fundraising is an area that often attracts intense scrutiny. How much of a donor's contributions actually are used to fund programs? What percentage of an organization's total budget comprises fundraising costs? Does each donor's contribution actually get used in the way the donor intended? You must be especially cautious when raising funds. Transparency, ethics, and integrity are of utmost importance.

Transparency

One of the hottest buzzwords in philanthropy these days is "transparency." Ensuring that your organization meets the highest ethical standards and that the public is fully aware of your organization policies and financial status is critical in today's world. To achieve transparency, the organization must have clearly documented ethical standards and corporate values, just as we have advised you to maintain clearly documented performance standards for all other areas of your business.

The Donor's Viewpoint

Donor-centered fundraising has become more than a buzzword in the field. It is mandatory if you want to retain donors.

You must always hold the donors' interests above your organization's needs.

What do donors expect from the organizations to whom they donate? Research has shown that donors are more aware than ever before of the importance of scrutinizing the nonprofit organizations to which they may consider contributing. What are some of the things they look for, and expect?

◆ Send donor-acknowledgment letters within twenty-four hours of receipt of the gift.

◆ Be sure you send your donors proper acknowledgment for IRS purposes, including the fact that they received no benefit in

Hints for Creating a Transparent Organization:

◆ Hire fundraising staff and consultants who are members of AFP or a similar professional organization with a code of ethics.

◆ Involve your organization in a Standards of Excellence Program, United Way accreditation, or other certification program for the organization itself.

◆ Ensure that your organization, *and* any consultants or professional solicitors that are hired by your organization, are registered in your state, if registration is required.

◆ Do not engage fundraising counsel or consultants who work on a percentage basis.

◆ Engage a CPA or other professional who is familiar with nonprofits to ensure that your 990 Form is completed accurately, reporting administrative and fundraising costs truthfully.

◆ Adhere to and publish the *Donor Bill of Rights*.

◆ Have a written gift-acceptance policy that outlines what types of gifts you will receive, how you will acknowledge and recognize those gifts, and how you will use and/or dispose of gifts received.

◆ Have a conflict-of-interest policy for your board and require all board members to sign a conflict-of-interest statement annually.

◆ Make sure you have a finance committee on the board with members who understand how to read financial statements.

◆ Be certain that your development staff, board, and other volunteers understand IRS regulations about "quid quo pro" and tax-deductibility issues and that donors are made aware of the deductibility or nondeductibility of gifts to the organization.

practical
tip

exchange for their donation, or the amount of the benefit they did receive (for example, fair market value of a dinner, round of golf, advertising given to sponsors, etc.).

◆ Be certain your 990 Form is accurate and provides examples of how donors' money is being used to directly benefit recipients of your services.

> Remember what we said earlier in this book. It costs six times more to find a new donor than it does to retain an existing donor.

◆ Publish donors' gifts in your annual report, unless they request anonymity.

◆ Always have a check box for the option to remain anonymous, and ask donors to print exactly how they *do* wish to be recognized if they are not making an anonymous gift.

◆ Use your website to provide donors with examples of how their gifts are being used.

◆ Be sure to use restricted gifts in the way the donor requests.

◆ Have a prudent investment policy for your funds.

◆ Ensure that knowledgeable people serve on your board budget and finance committee, and have an audit committee to ensure proper audits are done on a timely basis.

Donor Recognition

Donor recognition is also important. Public recognition is sought after, or at least accepted, by many individuals, most businesses, and many foundations. There are numerous ways you can recognize donors for their gifts. Depending on the size of the gift, you might consider naming a building or an area of a building, listing donors on your website, taking out an ad in the newspaper to thank donors, listing them in your newsletter, or holding donor-recognition events. Just make sure that you offer donors the option to remain anonymous and that you abide by their wishes if they choose to do so. You will find a sample Donor Recognition and Gift Policy in **Appendix A**.

Ethics

How do you develop a sense of ethics in your organization and in yourself? We would like to make a few suggestions:

◆ There are some great books available that discuss ethical judgments and ethical situations in fundraising. Check out sources like the AFP Bookstore for books on ethics in fundraising.

◆ If you believe in a particular faith system, this can be a help in developing your sense of morality and ethics. Every major religion holds certain moral principles that can help its members make sound ethical judgments.

◆ You can also enroll in a class in ethics and attend AFP programs on ethics.

◆ AFP also has an ethics committee that can answer questions about ethical issues.

You can help develop a sense of integrity by understanding ethics, morals, and donors' rights.

Although integrity is a quality that one either has or doesn't have, there are things you, as a development professional, can do to help develop your integrity. First, you should know, understand, and support the *AFP Code of Ethics and Standards of Professional Practice*. These documents will provide guidelines about what is ethical in the field of fundraising. Adherence to the *Donor Bill of Rights* is another step you can take to ensure that your organization holds the donor's interests above its own and that your staff holds the interests of the donor first, the organization second, and themselves last.

The Law

It is critical for nonprofits to comply with all federal, state, and local regulations. If your bylaws, policies, or procedures do not dovetail with the law, it's the law that always wins.

State Laws

Most states require nonprofits to register before engaging in fundraising. What you might not be aware of is that even if your state does not require registration, you might need to register in other states in which you are raising money. Be sure you are aware of and compliant with these laws. Penalties for failing to adhere to these laws can be very steep.

Another area that many people are unaware of is the registration requirement for fundraising consultants, including grantwriters, with whom you may be working.

Federal Laws

In the United States, the IRS not only grants nonprofit status but also imposes other regulations that apply to nonprofits. Some examples include the requirement to provide a letter to all donors who give $250 or more to a charity within a tax year. This letter must state that the donor did or did not receive anything in return for their contributions, and if the donor did receive goods or services, you must state the fair market value of those good or services.

While this book is not intended to provide legal or tax advice, we wanted to point out some of the pitfalls you can fall into if you are not aware of the legal, ethical, and moral issues surrounding fundraising activities. Read up on ethical and legal issues affecting nonprofits. You should always consult with your attorney or tax accountant about legal and tax issues.

Hiring a Consultant

After reading this book, you might decide you need help with certain aspects of your fundraising. While there are many factors that go into deciding whether a consultant is the right match for your organization, there are some things that fall under ethical and legal issues that we want to share with you.

Do You Need a Consultant—or a Staff Person?

The first thing you need to know is whether you are looking for a staff person to fill the role or if you need a consultant. If you need full-time work or someone to be on site on a regular basis, you probably need an employee rather than a consultant. Hiring a consultant is *not* a way to avoid paying benefits to employees. In fact, most states as well as the IRS have strict regulations about who is an employee and who is an outside contractor. Things such as supplying an office and equipment and supervising the person's work directly usually mean that person is considered an employee and you must pay employment taxes and possibly benefits. For a complete list of IRS guidelines, check the IRS website.

Know the Law and Ethics of Consulting

While some states do not require nonprofits or consultants to register in order to do fundraising campaigns and activities, most states do. So if your organization is headquartered in one of these states, you may need to check into state regulations regarding the hiring of a consultant.

Ask if the consultant is a member of the Association of Fundraising Professionals (AFP) or another association that carries a standard of ethics. And ask if the consultant is registered to do business in your state, assuming registration is required.

> The AFP code of ethics prohibits its members, including consultants, from working on a percentage-of-money-raised basis.
>
>
> important

The Written Contract

You should always have a written contract or letter of agreement with the consultant, signed by your organization and the consultant. This contract should outline fees and other expenses, a schedule of when fees are to be paid, a scope of work to be performed, a starting and ending date for the work, and a provision to extend or cancel the contract.

To Recap

◆ As we've stressed, this book is not meant to provide legal or tax advice, but it is important to be aware of these issues and how they affect your fundraising.

◆ Donor-centered fundraising demands that we value the interests of our donors above those of our organizations. It might be hard to think about turning away a large gift that your organization really needs, but if that gift is not in the best interest of our donors or consistent with our nonprofit's values, we must!

◆ Ethical decisions are not always black and white; there are a lot of gray areas. But there are tools to help you with ethical decision making.

◆ Document your ethical standards and values. Make sure staff and board are familiar with and understand them. An ounce of prevention is worth a pound of cure.

Chapter Seventeen

Using Your Assessment to Build an Effective Development Plan

IN THIS CHAPTER

···→ Building your plan to manage performance

···→ The big strategic issues examined by the Leaky Bucket study

···→ The four laws of performance management and why you should bother

···→ The Plan-Do-Check-Act cycle and effective reviews

Both of your coauthors can attest to this: Virtually every nonprofit professional we've ever met, or consulted with, or even spoken to, has acknowledged that fundraising is a challenge, at least some of the time, and an outright misery at least once or twice in their career. And that's why we wrote this book. We wanted to shine a light on the things that we know go wrong—and that the data tell us go wrong. We hope that we've been successful in showing you how to fix the problems in your fundraising organizations, but nothing beats avoiding a problem in the first place.

So this final chapter focuses on what you can do in the future to manage the performance of your fundraising efforts with forethought, using key business practices, performance indicators, and methods for review and analysis. There's nothing radical about our suggestions. They might strike you as common sense. But as the Leaky Bucket study has shown, so-called "common" sense is in short supply. It's downright *un*common.

Let's start with a few basic assumptions. Fail to take note of these, and your performance is likely to suffer.

◆ *Assumption #1:* If it's not written down, people will forget it, remember it wrong, or decide that it's okay to ignore it.

◆ *Assumption #2:* You can't rely on your memory. If you don't have information about your fundraising function carefully documented in sensible categories, all in one place, it doesn't matter how brilliant you are; you'll forget or overlook something.

◆ *Assumption #3:* Unless everybody is "on board" with the way you're going to run your fundraising, then nobody is on board.

◆ *Assumption #4:* If you don't celebrate the wins, you'll pay attention only to the losses.

◆ *Assumption #5:* It takes money, time, and consistent effort to make your fundraising successful. If you start it, drop it, and come back to it later, you're already losing out.

The Nine Commandments of Effective Fundraising

As we have said many times in this book, effective fundraising—fundraising that has nothing wrong with it—starts with planning. We've seen too many development plans that concentrate primarily on tactics and activities, going into great detail about the various events and activities scheduled for the coming year, with very little structure, attention to the basics, or useful measurements. In fact, that's the observation that led to the development of the Leaky Bucket Assessment in the first place—our suspicion that core business disciplines and performance metrics were MIA, missing in action, more often than you'd think.

So let's review the nine critical business practices that need to be put in place, in order for you to get the most out of your fundraising efforts with the least investment in time, money, and hassle:

◆ How you qualify (select) prospective funders

◆ How you acquire new funders

◆ How you retain current funders

- ◆ How you upgrade (up-sell and cross-sell) current donors

- ◆ What your standards are for fund diversification

- ◆ What your staff resources are for fundraising work

- ◆ How you measure fundraising performance

- ◆ What's in your fundraising tool kit

- ◆ How you respond to poor fundraising performance

Please take a look at your comprehensive development plan. If it doesn't honor the Nine Commandments, revise it. Or create a new one from scratch that does.

Commandment #1: Qualify Prospective Funders With a Well-Documented Set Of Criteria.

In our study to date, the overwhelming majority of respondents—an astounding 76 percent—stated that they had either no criteria, or undocumented preferences for qualifying donor prospects. That's a huge failing. Without documented preferences in place, you and your team might well flail about, wasting precious time on the wrong opportunities, prospects that don't have much to offer or are going to end up making you sorry you got their money in the first place.

To create a development plan that really works for you, establish the criteria for qualifying prospects right away. Write up an ideal-funder profile for donors, grantmakers, and corporate relations. Make sure your profile includes qualitative information such as values, motivations for giving and the like, as well as the standard demographics, wealth profile, and information about giving history.

These funding profiles are your benchmarks for discriminating between funding prospects with high potential for bringing you long-term income, moderate potential, or very little potential.

Once you have documented your ideal-funder profiles, police yourself and your team. Find out whether you're pursuing prospects that are a good match to the profile. If you're not, find out why. There is no meaningful excuse for investing lots of time in prospects that don't justify the effort.

Commandment #2: Establish Targets for Acquiring New Funders.

Although we are well aware that it costs a lot more to bring in a new donor than it does to retain one, you'll always need to acquire new sources of funding, for two reasons. First, you can't retain every donor. Second, you can't grow significantly without additional donors.

Sounds good, right? But once again, the data show that a majority of respondents have no standards or performance targets for acquiring new donors, or they have preferences but no such targets. Fully 65 percent of respondents chose one of those two options. A preference means "We know it's a good idea, but we don't bother to keep track of it."

In order to bring in a desirable number of new funders every year, you must have specific, well-crafted methods and campaigns. Even more important, you must have documented performance targets including total number of new funders per income category plus total amounts of income raised. And of course, once you've set up those methods and documented those performance indicators, you've got to keep track of performance against your plan on a regular basis. Regular reviews of performance against plan keep the team focused on the desired result and give insights into what's working, what's not, and what you can improve.

Commandment #3: Document Targets for Retaining Current Funders.

As we've said, it's easier to retain a donor than it is to acquire a new one. So how come so few nonprofits actually have standards or performance targets for donor retention? Our data show that 66 percent of all respondents had *no* standards for donor retention, or were encouraged to retain funders but had no documented targets or practices. Being "encouraged" to retain donors is a lot like "having preferences" for acquiring new ones; it doesn't work. It's a weak motivator and doesn't hold anyone accountable for results.

Donor retention is too important to tolerate such a lazy attitude. Establish a donor-retention target for every funding category. If you have a large base of grants, you'll want to know what proportion of grants will come to the end of their granting cycle in the current year and which ones you'll want to replace with new grants. Write down either how many grants you'll aim to replace or how much income from new grants you'll need to produce (why not both?). For your major and individual donors, calculate the percentage that you're most likely to lose in spite of your best efforts. People move, lose interest in your cause, go broke, or die. Maybe next year you'll only lose 7 percent, but maybe 10 or 15 percent is more realistic. Then make the remainder your performance target. State this remainder as your retention target: "Retain at least 85 percent of all funding sources at the same or higher giving levels."

Calculate a specific performance target. "More" is not a target. "Between x percent and y percent" is a weak target, while "z percent" is dandy. You're better off with a specific, defined, documented target. The Nonprofit Police do not take you to jail if you miss or exceed your targets.

Commandment #4: Establish Performance Objectives for Upgrading Current Donors.

Once you have obtained gifts and grants, you now need to steward these relationships. Stewardship refers to the array of tasks and activities that maintain healthy relationships with your donors and other funders. The first desirable outcome of stewardship is, of course, ensuring that donors will give again this year at no less than the rate they gave to you last year.

But stewardship has a secondary objective, which is to increase the size and number of gifts your donors produce. And that takes campaigns to up-sell and cross-sell your donors.

Well, guess what? About 77 percent of our study participants said that they either had no targets for developing their donors through up-selling and cross-selling, or that they were encouraged to do so but had no performance targets. Only 5 percent stated that they had definite performance targets and that they also conducted specific campaigns for the purpose of up-selling or cross-selling their donors.

For heaven's sake, if you want to make something happen, establish a SMART objective! Remember that the performance objective needs to be S—specific and M—measurable. "Increase the average size of all individual donations by 10 percent by December 31 of next year" is a specific and measurable objective. And you can track performance against it every month. Once you've locked such objectives and metrics into your plan, you've got the most effective way to track performance.

*Commandment #5: Establish and Maintain Standards for
Fund Diversification.*

Fund diversification seems to work better in organizations with more
mature development offices. We were glad to see that. About 49 percent
of our sample said that they got their income from a variety of sources but
still needed to improve balance, while another 16 percent said that their
diversification programs were well balanced.

But this still leaves about 9 percent with only a single funding source and
about 25 percent who get most of their income from a single category such
as grants.

Fund diversification is another one of those strategic issues that deserves
more attention than it's getting. Nonprofits that tolerate low levels of
fund diversification have put their future at risk. Government money
is capricious, foundations are conservative in their giving policies, and
individual and corporate donors must balance a variety of interests and
ways of coping with economic fluctuations. Striving for ever-higher levels
of diversification is a basic survival strategy.

Even if the ink on your agency's 501(c)(3) is still wet, it's not too soon for
you to work on your strategies for diversification. Among other things,
achieving bulletproof levels can take years and require a variety of skills,
techniques, and campaign tactics to reach your objectives.

In order to choose targets for fund diversification, first calculate all
income by category. How much comes from individual donations, from
corporations, from grants, from fee-for-service income, etc. Keep the
number of categories as small as possible (i.e., don't have a category for
left-handed individual donors and a separate one for right-handed donors;
just mix all donors into one category). Once you can see your income
by these broader categories, decide by how much you'd like to change
things in the coming year. It's okay to choose modest targets for changing
the proportions of funding diversification. Modest changes are not only
acceptable, but they also tend to be easier to achieve.

Commandment #6: Provide Adequate Staff Resources for
Fundraising Work.

Fundraising, or development, or advancement is professional work that
requires time, dedication, persistence, and expertise. Although it's fine
to include some volunteers in the effort, at the end of the day, there is a
direct correlation between adequate fundraising *results* and adequate
fundraising *staff*.

Regrettably, there is a tendency to wait too long before staffing up the
development office, especially in human service agencies. If you expect
your executive director to do all the fundraising work, something is going
to suffer. Most likely, it's going to be the fundraising. Twenty-five percent
of our sample shows that the ED is doing all the fundraising work, and
another 31 percent or so have one person in addition to the ED. We were
happy to see that a healthy 24 percent employ a fully staffed development
shop with a CDO, multiple staff members, and help from the board.

We would like to see more nonprofits hire more development staff earlier
in their evolution. Although the tendency among human service agencies
is to hire technical or clinical or program staff long before they hire
development professionals, we would encourage those agencies to think
twice. The sooner they can produce sustainable income, the sooner they'll
be able to staff up for other purposes. Doing the conventional thing may
mean that the agency is running a budget that's much tighter than it needs
to be.

Where other "commandments" make it easy to establish performance
targets and other standards, standards around staffing are somewhat more
elusive. One of the most desirable practices to adopt is that of regular
capacity reviews of the development team. Are development officers so
busy managing grants that they don't have time to seek new ones? Are they
so busy maintaining relationships with major donors that they can't find
new ones or come up with ideas for cross-selling? Are they so overloaded
with events that they have no time to spend on major gift work? First,
determine whether capacity could be improved with better efficiency. But
if not, the CDO and/or CEO of the organization should build a business
case for adding staff.

Since by now you have already decided to adopt and document specific targets for acquiring new funders and for retaining, up-selling, and cross-selling current donors, if performance in these categories either declines or levels off, reviewing the capacity of staff resources is in order.

Commandment #7: Utilize a Range of Metrics to Manage Fundraising Performance.

At the risk of a broad generalization, nonprofits tend to lag behind their for-profit counterparts in terms of the ways they use metrics to manage income. For example, the most widely used measurement in both sales and fundraising is "total income." But only about 63 percent of Leaky Bucket study participants use it. We anticipated seeing something like 99 percent! Why don't all nonprofits specify a goal or target for total income?

The second most common metric used was "income by category," where the agency would have a target for grants income, individual-donor income, and so on. We also anticipated seeing a very high percentage of respondents choosing that metric, but only about half (about 47 percent) did so.

There are two huge problems with these findings. First, it suggests that far too many nonprofit organizations will wing it when it comes to raising money. Think about it. Instead of saying, "It's going to take us such and such an amount of money to achieve our mission," the agency tacitly says, "Let's see how much we can earn, and then we'll decide how much to spend."

Second, those income metrics are so-called trailing indicators. As we explained back in **Chapter Three**, trailing indicators, while valuable, come in after the process is complete and do not reveal any inefficiencies or obstacles in the process itself.

We have reviewed a number of trailing indicators in this chapter that you should adopt and make part of your development plan. They include total number of new funders, total number of retained donors, total numbers of donors, and amounts of income produced by up-selling and cross-selling, among others.

But let's not overlook the highly diagnostic and revealing leading indicators.

The first leading indicator we suggest is "total opportunity income in the pipeline." Opportunities that you carry in your pipeline are *potential* income, not realized income. You will always carry more potential income in your pipeline than the total amount of income you will actually collect. So assign a "pipeline multiplier" target. If you don't currently have a baseline for calculating the multiplier, simply guess. We tend to recommend a pipeline multiplier of three for agencies with no defined baseline. But choose whatever seems right to you, then adjust it based on firm data. If your income target is $1 million and your pipeline multiplier is a factor of three, then your target for "total opportunity income in the pipeline" is $3 million.

Other useful leading indicators can include opportunity-stage definitions, such as:

◆ Total number of new opportunities entering the pipeline this month

◆ Total number of opportunities in the pipeline that have moved from "just entered" to "accepted a proposal for a gift or grant"

◆ Total number of opportunities in the pipeline that have moved from "accepted a proposal" to "reviewed proposal with you and discussed terms, size, or other matters"

Use your imagination. If you can think of other leading indicators that are both diagnostic (revealing) and easy to capture, try using them for a few months or a year to see if they help you perform better and more efficiently.

Commandment #8: Keep a Complete Fundraising Tool Kit.

Set up your fundraising tool kit ahead of time. It's easier than finding out you need something that you don't have when you're sitting across the desk from a major donor prospect. Remember, if the brochure, or flyer, or case statement, or annual report isn't fabulous, you can always improve it later. There's a big difference between having something useful but not perfect and having nothing at all.

This was another area where our study revealed some unexpected, and disappointing, findings. First, the good news: 45 percent said they had a strategic plan with fundraising goals and objectives, and 56 percent said they had some form of donor-management software, even if it was just a spreadsheet. (Be aware that a spreadsheet will not provide you with the donor history that you need to build donor relationships.) That's better than half, but not by much. Although you're not likely to carry your strategic plan with you on donor visits, you need to know what it says. Ditto for donor-management software. But why aren't the numbers higher? If you turn the study numbers upside down, we see that 55 percent do *not* have a strategic plan with fundraising goals (groan), and 44 percent lack any form of donor-management technology.

Perhaps the most troubling finding of all has to do with the case statement. Only 22 percent of study participants reported that they have an up-to-date case statement. When we reviewed these findings at a trade-association meeting, where most attendees were development professionals from larger nonprofits, they said things such as "We know we need to have one, but who has time?" and "We asked the program directors to update it, and they never gave it back." This is an elaborate version of "the dog ate my homework." There's virtually no single document that's more meaningful to the fundraising effort, at least no document that you'd use with prospective funders, than your case statement, and there are thousands of guidelines, training programs, and templates for creating them. Fix it!

Manage this commandment by including a regularly scheduled review of the fundraising tool kit at least once every six months, at which time the case statements and other pertinent documents should be revised and refreshed if necessary, or kept as is.

Commandment #9: Manage Your Response When Fundraising Performance Falls Below Desired Levels.

If fundraising produces undesirable results, it's not helpful to run around in a frenzy, throwing more events, and chasing more grant applications. Maybe you *do* need more events or more grants, but unless you have very good evidence that you *need* more, and very good reasons for *doing* more, it's better to avoid such risky and costly tactics. Since the board so often recommends "more events," staff may find it difficult to say no. That's why you need a development plan with powerful, robust metrics for maintaining excellent performance, with thoughtful alternatives for managing things when they're below par.

And yet, our data shows that 49 percent of respondents said they would hold more fundraising events if results were poor, and 49 percent would write more grant applications. Both of these are tactics with high costs and only moderate returns.

Put more faith into methods for improving performance with lower costs and higher returns, such as board/staff training and improving the case statement.

But the all-time best way to manage undesirable fundraising results is to prevent them. You'll do this if you track key fundraising performance indicators with care and consistency, so that you get "early warnings" if things are going downhill. Paying attention to your indicators will point out where you could improve internal efficiencies, when to hire additional staff or contractors, or what other things you might do to enhance capacity. Perhaps all it takes is testing alternative appeal letters, improving the navigation of your website, or tweaking your Facebook page.

If such initiatives do not adequately address the problem, think about training your staff members. At the very least, encourage staff members to pursue credentials such as the CFRE, pay for their membership in trade associations like the Association of Fundraising Professionals, and so on. We have seen a number of clients establish a sort of internal book club, where all executives, or everybody on the fundraising team, will read a book on management or fundraising practices and discuss the tenets of the book during regular staff meetings.

The Four Laws of Performance Management

When you want to run a really top-notch fundraising organization, it's not just what you do and how you do it. As important as that stuff is, it's still not the whole picture. It also requires ways to manage the performance of the development effort. The science of performance management has grown up a lot in recent years; these days you can even get a PhD in the field. Some people call it "process management" or "process improvement," but at the end of the day, they all mean the same thing. Here are four simple "laws" of performance management, and if you can memorize them and put them to work in your organization, we (Linda and Ellen) will give you our equivalent of a PhD. Here they are:

◆ *You can't manage it if you can't measure it.* And you can't improve it if you can't measure it. So if "it" is worth doing, then figure out how to measure it. Review **Chapter Four** on metrics for more ideas.

◆ *What you measure is what you get.* If you're going to measure it, you're going to get it. If you want your people to make lots of phone calls, measure phone calls. But if you want your people to cultivate new donors, or collect a certain amount of money, then don't measure your phone calls! Measure number of new donors and amount of money—if that's what you want to produce.

◆ *You can't figure out much by using a single measurement.* Well, you wouldn't build a house if the only measurement you had was for the bathroom window! If you measure only income or number of donors, you're missing out on other important insights that will tell you something about the health of your process.

◆ *If the only thing you measure happens after the process is complete, you haven't learned much about the process.* Inspecting finished goods after they come off the assembly line is expensive. If the goods are defective, you have wasted unrecoverable time, raw materials, and money to produce something you'll throw into the garbage. In fundraising, if you measure only the trailing end of the process, you don't know where you wasted time, pursued a dead end, or spent money you didn't need to spend in order to reach your target.

Familiarize yourself with these concepts, and you'll quickly become a more effective planner. And get better results.

Changing the Way You Run Your Team Meetings

Throughout this book, you've seen recommendations for how to do fundraising tasks more efficiently and more effectively. You've learned how to create a development plan that can work to improve results and maintain accountability. The very last piece of the puzzle is for you to learn how to keep yourself and everyone else on the team focused on success.

And it's a lot easier than you might think.

Schedule regular team meetings to review and analyze results. The optimum team-meeting schedule is about an hour once a month. Focus the entire meeting on a review of performance against plan. The formula for successful meetings goes like this:

◆ Present a report that shows actual results against planned results. Do not, repeat, *do not* collect results data at the meeting, but put it together beforehand. Separate data from anecdotes in this report. Show just the key performance targets, current monthly performance against target, and total year-to-date performance against target. Use exactly the same reporting format *every month*.

◆ Have team members review findings quietly for a few moments.

◆ Ask for observations by saying things such as "What do we see?" or "What's going on?" Do not allow conversations about what went wrong, who's to blame, or even "These numbers are lousy." Instead, you want people to say things like "I see we're up/down/sideways this month."

◆ Ask which results are satisfactory and which results ought to be improved.

◆ For satisfactory results, ask your people "How can we lock in similar results in the coming months?"

◆ For results that people agree should be changed, ask "What might have happened upstream to produce these results?" In other words, try to figure out if the problem could be prevented next time around by doing something different in an earlier step. Do not allow the conversation to devolve into arguments about whose fault it was or who is to blame; these conversations go nowhere and make everybody miserable in the process.

◆ Always ask "Do we want to keep the same target or change it?" You may always adjust targets up or down, depending on your findings. Avoid changing targets just because you're in the mood, or because it seems easier to reach a lower target. Challenge yourself to find innovative ways of reaching the higher target instead!

Before you run campaigns, cultivate donors, or do anything else to raise money, create a comprehensive development plan that covers the nine core strategic issues or "commandments" that produce optimum fundraising results. If your plan takes these issues into account, you will outperform your peers and competitors with your consistent attention to transparency (you can see what's going on), accountability (you can keep yourself and your team focused on what needs to be done), and continuous improvement (you always find something you can do to raise income, lower costs, or find innovations).

Lock in these new concepts by understanding that part of your leadership job is to manage the performance of the development effort. And that means more than simply doing the activities of fundraising. It means having clear, careful measurements, success targets, benchmarks, guidelines, rules, processes, and reports that make it easy to wrap your arms around the whole thing and make it better month after month and year after year.

Finally, we suggest a few practical methods you can use to get and keep your team focused on improving performance continuously. Change your agenda from one of reporting by anecdote to one of analyzing for the sake of continuous improvement. The rewards of this approach are many, and you'll see them begin to emerge quickly.

To Recap

♦ *Commandment #1:* Qualify prospective funders with a well-documented set of criteria.

♦ *Commandment #2:* Establish and document targets for numbers of new funders acquired as well as amount of income acquired.

♦ *Commandment #3:* Establish and document targets for retaining current funders as well as amount of income retained.

♦ *Commandment #4:* Establish and document performance objectives for upgrading current donors through up-selling and cross-selling.

♦ *Commandment #5:* Establish and maintain standards for fund diversification.

◆ *Commandment #6:* Provide adequate staff resources for fundraising work.

◆ *Commandment #7:* Utilize a range of metrics to manage fundraising performance, because if you can't measure it, you can't manage it.

◆ *Commandment #8:* Keep and frequently update a complete fundraising tool kit so you can fix things *before* they break.

◆ *Commandment #9:* Manage your response when fundraising performance falls below desired levels.

Appendix A

Resources, Links, and Comments Organized by Chapter

Chapter One: The Leaky Bucket Assessment

See **Appendix B** for a complete copy of the Leaky Bucket Assessment for Effective Fundraising as well as a link to the online assessment tool.

There are a number of other tools you may use to assess your development program, your readiness for a capital campaign, and more at www.cvfundraising.com/resources/development.

Chapter Two: Evaluating Your Fundraising Infrastructure

Sample Gift Recognition Policies

Mandate

Every donation to XYZ Organization, regardless of size or value, will be duly recognized and recorded.

Purpose

◆ To acknowledge donor contributions.

◆ To build lasting relationships with donors inviting further contributions and providing reciprocal positive exposure for their philanthropy.

- ◆ To advise donors how their generous contributions are utilized.

- ◆ To stimulate interest and support among potential donors.

Definitions

Donor: An individual or organization who agrees to donate a one-time or renewed amount over a specified period of time.

Gift: Can include monetary gifts or gifts of property or services, which include, but are not limited to RRSPs, insurance benefits, stocks, bonds, gifts-in-kind (i.e., services, computer equipment, tickets, etc.), and real estate. The transfer is voluntary and without the expectation of return. All *nonmonetary* gift donations must first be communicated to XYZ Organization.

Other Policies

Responsibility for the general administration of the policy rests with the development office of XYZ Organization.

All donors will be acknowledged within thirty days of their donation.

Tax receipts will be provided for donations that meet the IRS definition of a charitable donation.

Donors wishing to remain anonymous will be respected; however, donors must indicate their wish to remain anonymous at the time of donation.

In respect of donor confidentiality, XYZ Organization will not disclose donor information to outside sources under any circumstances.

All donations will be adequately recorded and logged.

The level of donor recognition is determined at the time of contribution or upon the agreement of an ongoing contribution.

In the event a donor recognition level must be changed, equal recognition will be arranged and communicated to donors at that level.

Special requests for unique donor recognition will be considered if put forth by the donor; however, discretion is ultimately left with XYZ Organization.

Governance Policies

For examples of effective governance policies, take a look at *Reinventing Your Board,* by John and Miriam Mayhew Carver, which lists samples of policies related to the Policy Governance® model.

Another excellent source for policies and standards covering virtually all aspects of nonprofit management is the Standards for Excellence Institute, a project of Maryland Nonprofits. Their Standards for Excellence Code includes eight Guiding Principles and fifty-five performance benchmarks. For more information, visit the website of the Standards for Excellence Institute: www.standardsforexcellenceinstitute.org/dnn/TheCode.aspx.

Chapter Three: Technology, The Glue that Holds It All Together

Services for Email Marketing

There are two types of email marketing systems. One is a service where you store your email subscription list online and send your emails, newsletters, and announcements directly from the site of the service provider. A major advantage of such systems is that the service provider handles all the work required to "white list" or gain permission to deliver emails to the in-boxes of the recipients. Best-known providers of this type, at time of publication, include the following:

- Constant Contact

- iContact

- MailDog

- MailChimp

The second type is the software application that you integrate directly into your donor or constituent database. This type of application allows you to "tag" your contacts for certain mailing purposes and send your emails directly from your own system. The major advantage of this type of application is that you have to update only one database. You never have to worry that your e-newsletter subscription list is out of sync with your internal constituent database. Vertical Response is one such application.

Blogging Systems

The two most popular blogging systems, at time of publication, are WordPress and Blogspot. Both of these are free (again, at time of publication). They are simple to use, from a technology perspective. You can also get lots of advice on using blogs and blogging effectively from both providers and other sources. Just enter the term "how to blog" on your preferred search engine.

Social Media

The most popular social networking tools (as of 2013) are Facebook, Twitter, LinkedIn, Google+, YouTube, and Pinterest. If you don't use or plan to use videos, then you don't need to bother with YouTube.

A good site to visit for advice on utilizing social media for nonprofit organizations is www.socialmedianonprofits.com.

Donor-Management Software

TechSoup (www.techsoup.org) has several articles, publications and other resources to help you compare donor-management software products. Visit this page: www.techsoup.org/learningcenter/databases, or simply explore the site.

And don't forget that TechSoup also offers nonprofits free or heavily discounted prices on many technology products.

Chapter Eight: Human Resources—The Role of Your Board

Sample template for requesting contact information from board members:

Name of board member: _____

Corporate contact: _____

Company: _____

Title: _____

Phone: _____

Email address: _____

Relationship: _____

When do you plan to contact this individual? _____

Board/Volunteer Recruitment Packets

Board Recruitment Packet	Development Committee Recruitment Packet	Fundraising Volunteer Recruitment Packet
Bylaws of the organization		
Bylaws of the organization Board member position description	Development committee member position description	Volunteer position description
List of board meeting dates with times and locations	List of development committee meeting dates with times and locations	List of committee meeting dates with times and locations
List of current board members	List of current development committee members and list of current board members	List of other volunteers involved in this committee or project and list of current board members
Your organization's case for support	Your organization's case for support	Your organization's case for support
Your development plan	Your development plan	
		Timeline of project or campaign on which you are asking the volunteer to work
Organization budget for current fiscal year		
Any other information about your organization that might be helpful to the prospective board member	Any other information about your organization that might be helpful to the prospective development committee member	Any other information about your organization that might be helpful to the prospective volunteer

Chapter Ten: Too Many Eggs, Too Few Baskets—Why Fund Diversification Is So Important

This chart shows national average for philanthropic giving in the United States from individuals, corporations, and foundations, excluding earned income and government funding.

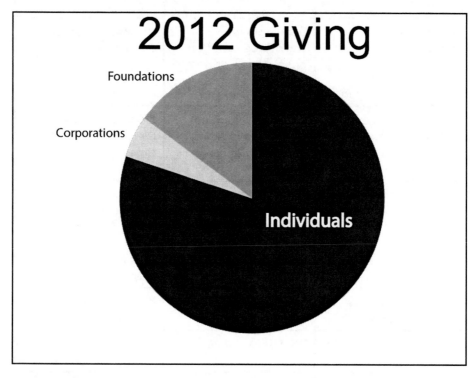

Use the following template to analyze your current levels of fund diversification.

Funding Stream	Total Dollars for Current Year	Percentage of Total Income (approximate)
Private Foundation Grants		
Government Grants & Appropriations		
Corporate Sponsorships		
Individual Donations		
Major Gifts		
Earned Income		

Draw a pie chart that represents the proportions.

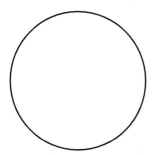

Repeat the exercise, showing how you would like to modify your diversification twelve months from now.

Funding Stream	Total Dollars for Current Year	Percentage of Total Income (approximate)
Private Foundation Grants		
Government Grants & Appropriations		
Corporate Sponsorships		
Individual Donations		
Major Gifts		
Earned Income		

Draw another pie chart representing the desired changes.

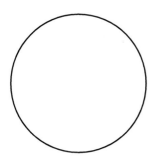

You may also obtain an automated version of this template from Bristol Strategy Group. Visit www.bristolstrategygroup.com/resources/fund-diversification-calculator.

Chapter Twelve: Special Event Planning Checklist

Checklist for Assets

What do we already have in the organization to make this fundraising project a success? What factors should we consider in choosing an event?

People

- ❑ Leaders—their time and talents

- ❑ Members with experience with this kind of event

- ❑ Total number of members who will work

- ❑ Total number of members who will attend or contribute

- ❑ Possible allies and new members who will get involved

- ❑ Staff

Money

- ❑ Seed money available for the event—from treasury, loan, advance sales

- ❑ When will we have to send the money? When will the money come in? What is our break-even point (income = expenses)?

- ❑ Who will handle the money coming in? Who will control the money going out?

- ❑ Bank—will we need a separate account? Do we need any special arrangements to handle lots of cash?

Time

- ❑ How much time does the organization want to spend fundraising? Is there a way to shorten it?

- ❑ Are there any major conflicts in the organization's calendar? The community calendar?

- ❑ How much staff time do we want to allocate to this project?

- ❑ If this event is to be repeated annually, is this the best time of the year for it?

- ❑ What consideration should we make for bad weather (e.g., an alternative snow/rain date, inside location, or insurance)?

Checklist for Goals

❑ What do we want to achieve from this project?

❑ Amount of money, net. Percentage of annual budget

❑ Number of people involved. Where and how?

❑ Number of leadership roles possible

❑ Number of new members brought in

❑ Experience. Which skills will be learned? What do we want to learn for the next event, and for this event next year?

❑ Who will take the leadership positions?

❑ Who will challenge the elected leaders?

❑ What will be the publicity generated? How much, what kind, where?

Special Event Analysis

1. Rank each current or proposed event on Part I of the form. For example, if the event takes less than twenty-five staff hours, give it a 5.

2. Total up the points and rate the event:

   ◆ 35—The Perfect Event (Don't we all wish?)

   ◆ 30–34—An excellent event; definitely worth keeping

   ◆ 25–29—A good event; probably worth keeping but may need some minor changes

   ◆ 20–24—A reasonably good event; may be worth keeping but should evaluate ways to improve

   ◆ Less than 20—Need to consider dropping this event or making serious changes

Special Event Activity Analysis

Fundraising Activity	Date	Cost (Est.)	Income (Est.)	Profit $000s (Est.)	Staff Hours Req'd.	Vol. Hours Req'd	New Names Acq'd	Taps Large Donors	Builds Aware-Ness	Risk Factor	Bonds Donors	Total	Ranking
					<25=5 25-100=3 100>=1	<100=5 100-200=3 200>=1	200+ =5 100-199=3 0-99=1	10+ =5 5-9=3 1-5=1	High=5 Med=3 Low=1	Low=5 Med=3 High=1	High=5 Med=3 Low=1		

3. Please keep in mind that this evaluation is subjective. For example, if an event is raising $1 million but requires a lot of staff and volunteer time, it is probably worth keeping despite a lower rating.

Guidelines for State Registration

Some resources to help with state registration include:

- ◆ Affinity Fundraising Registration: www.fundraisingregistration.com

- ◆ Clearly Compliant: www.clearlycompliant.com

- ◆ Copilevitz & Canter LLP: www.copilevitz-canter.com

- ◆ Labyrinth Inc.: www.labyrinthinc.com

- ◆ Montgomery, McCracken, Walker & Rhoads, LLP: www.mmwr.com

- ◆ Perlman & Perlman LLP: www.perlmanandperlman.com

- ◆ Webster, Chamberlain & Bean LLP: www.wc-b.com

The *Nonprofit Consultant Playbook*, published in 2013 by CharityChannel Press, includes a comprehensive table describing all the registration requirements and links for fundraiser registration by state.

You will also find additional guidance for registering your fundraising consulting practice at your state department of corporations.

Organizational Life Cycles

Like all other business entities (nonprofit, public sector and for-profit), nonprofit organizations go through a "life cycle," and they need different things at different stages.

Margaret Guellich's model is very useful:

Organizational Life Cycles

Family Life

Infancy ⟹	School ⟹	Teenage ⟹	Adult
Dependent	Social	Testing	Maturing

Organizational Life

Informal Entrepreneurial ⟹	Family Bureaucratic ⟹	Expansion Decentralize ⟹	Coordinate Groups/Committees ⟹	Participation Matrix Structure
New born	10 years	15 years	20 year	25+ years
Unstable	Stable	Stable	Stable	Unstable
Simple	Complex	Simple	Complex	Complex
Growth	Growth	Diversity	Maturing	Break Offs
Needs Direction	No harmony	Lack of Control	Adaptation	Growing Pains

Where are you?

Another effective model was designed by Dr. Ichak Adizes, a global expert on managing organizational change. Visit the Adizes Institute website for more information on Adizes Maturity Model, www.adizes.com.

Appendix B

The Leaky Bucket Assessment for Effective Fundraising

The Leaky Bucket Assessment for Effective Fundraising identifies the level of maturity of nine fundamental business practices that either contribute to or detract from the productivity, efficiency, and sustainability of a nonprofit's fund-development function. It was inspired by Ellen's observation that productivity tends to "leak" out of fundraising organizations in ways we don't notice until the pipes burst and there's a crisis.

Assessments are scored and ranked in four equal groups ranging from lowest to highest:

- ◆ Leaking Like a Sieve!

- ◆ Call the Productivity Help Line!

- ◆ Time for Preventive Productivity Maintenance!

- ◆ Watertight!

If you would like to complete the online version of the assessment, which is scored automatically, you may do so by visiting www.bristolstrategygroup.com/nonprofit-leakybucket.

Six Questions to Assess Your Agency's Current Fundraising Practices (all questions are required)

1. Choose your agency's standard practices for qualifying prospective grantors, donors, corporate sponsors.

   a. No standards; we just go after what looks good to us.

   b. Preferences but no documented standards; we go after grants whose granting guidelines match our needs.

   c. We have profiles for each funding category based on their capacity to give, grant guidelines, or giving history.

   d. We have documented profiles for each funding category; they include donor motivation and preferences as well as the standard facts.

   Comments: _____

2. Choose your agency's standard practices for acquiring new funding sources (grants, donors, corporate sponsors, etc.).

   a. No standard practices or targets; we just try as hard as we can every year.

   b. We encourage acquiring new funders but don't set specific targets.

   c. We set targets for acquiring new-donor gifts and grants based on income only.

   d. We set targets for number of new donors per funding category as well as amount of dollars raised from new sources.

   Comments: _____

3. Choose your agency's standard practices for retaining current donors.

    a. Our agency has no standard practices or targets for retaining donors or renewing grants.

    b. Our agency encourages donor/grantor retention but does not assign specific targets for doing so.

    c. Our agency sets specific performance targets for retaining donors and grantors.

    d. Our agency has standard, documented practices for retaining current donors that include total dollars raised from current donors, and number of donors retained from prior years.

Comments: _____

4. Choose your agency's standard practices for "up-selling" and "cross-selling" your current funders.

    a. We have no standard practices; we just try hard every year.

    b. We encourage development of current donors, but don't assign any specific targets or run any fundraising programs to do so.

    c. We set targets every year for increasing the size of gifts, extension of grants, etc.

    d. We set specific targets and goals for "up-selling" and "cross-selling" major donors, corporate partners and grantors, with specific campaigns for doing so.

Comments: _____

5. Choose your agency's standard practices for funding diversification.

   a. Most of our funding comes from a small number of sources, especially state or local agencies. We don't think about funding diversification very much.

   b. Most of our funding comes from one category, like grants. We have only a few other types of funders (corporate sponsors, individual donors) and need to work on this.

   c. We get funding from a variety of sources, although the level of funding diversity is still not balanced well.

   d. Our funding is well balanced among a variety of funding sources, with no single funder accounting for more than a defined proportion of total income.

   Comments: _____

6. Choose your agency's standard practices regarding staff resources for fundraising.

   a. We have no fundraising staff; our executive director does all the fundraising, operational, and program work.

   b. We have at least one fundraising staff person (or contractor) full time or part time in addition to the executive director.

   c. We have two or more staff members or contractors who do fundraising work and also support fundraising efforts of our ED and board members.

   d. We have a development director plus staff dedicated to fundraising. We also get our board and ED involved.

   Comments: _____

Three Questions on How Your Agency Measures Fundraising Performance

7. How does your agency measure fundraising performance today? Check all that apply.

    a. Overall income compared with our fundraising goal

    b. Income for each funding category compared with our goal for that category

    c. Number of times we visit with donors, corporate sponsors, etc.

    d. Number of grant applications or donor proposals we produce

    e. Growth of donor database compared with our goal for database size

    f. None of the above

    Comments: _____

8. Does your agency have a comprehensive fundraising tool kit? Check all items that your agency actually uses on a regular basis.

    a. Strategic plan with specific fundraising goals and objectives

    b. Fundraising plan with targets for funding diversification

    c. Prospect profiles for qualifying donors, grantors and/or corporate sponsors

    d. Donor management spreadsheet or software application

    e. Formal case statement

    f. Standard solicitation letters, presentation templates, and other aids to cultivating donors and corporate partners

    g. Solicitor training for staff and board members involved in prospect cultivation

    h. None of the above

Comments: _____

9. Check the following techniques that your agency uses when fundraising performance runs below desired levels. Please be honest with your answers. Choose as many as you wish.

    a. Fire our development director.

    b. Increase number of fundraising activities or events.

    c. Write more grant applications.

    d. Provide staff/board solicitor training.

    e. Improve or update our case statement, presentation formats, solicitation scripts and the like.

    f. Define our ideal donor profiles; use them to qualify prospects.

    g. None of the above.

Index